The Leadership Mirror

THE LEADERSHIP MIRROR

Look Inward. Lead Outward.

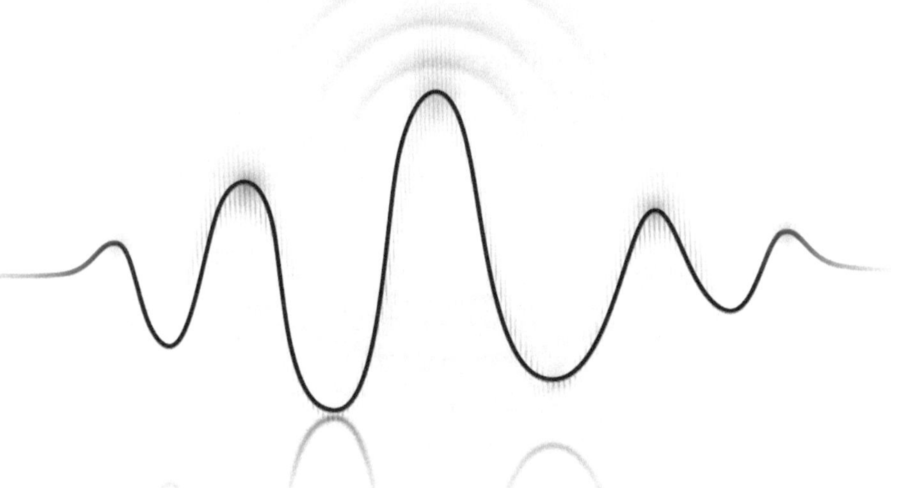

Julie McManus

Identifiers

Paperback (Perfect Bound) ISBN: 978-1-970642-07-0
Hardcover (Case Laminate) ISBN: 978-1-970642-08-7
Hardcover (Dust Jacket) ISBN: 978-1-970642-09-4
eBook (EPUB) ISBN: 978-1-970642-10-0

Published by Skinny Brown Dog Media
www.SkinnyBrownDogMedia.com
Author: Julie McManus
Publisher of Record: Skinny Brown Dog Media
Language: English

Permissions & Licensing

For bulk purchases, international translation, audiobook rights, or AI/licensing inquiries, please contact:
Skinny Brown Dog Media
www.SkinnyBrownDogMedia.com
info@SkinnyBrownDogMedia.com

Printed in the United States of America

Dedication

For the next generation of leaders
who understand that real influence begins within.

May you be bold enough to examine your blind spots,
steady enough to grow through them,
and generous enough to lift others as you rise.

And to the many leaders and teams
who let me experiment, stumble, recover, and refine this work,
thank you for shaping the mirror alongside me.

What People Are Saying about *The Leadership Mirror*

"What Julie McManus has created in The Leadership Mirror is nothing short of an ignition switch for personal responsibility and courageous leadership. She challenges you, supports you, and hands you the tools to step into the version of yourself you've been avoiding or postponing. This book is real, relatable, and packed with actionable insight. Leaders who are serious about connection, clarity, and getting real business results need this on their desk, not their shelf."

— Anne Bonney,
Keynote Speaker, Emcee &
Host of Dancing in the
Discomfort Zone Podcast

"Reading The Leadership Mirror felt like sitting across the table from Julie again. After twenty-five years of working together, I know exactly how she shows up, and her voice comes through in every chapter. She is clear-spoken, honest, and unafraid to challenge a leader who needs to take a real look at what is going on.

Julie has an uncommon ability to diagnose what is blocking progress, whether at the project level or across an entire culture. Her empathy is one of her greatest strengths, and so is her focus. She sees the big strategic picture while also giving full attention to the people doing the work. Leaders at every level will benefit from the practical wisdom in this book."

— Jeff Poore,
Senior Executive and
Former Colleague

"For more than two decades in the U.S. Air Force, I had the opportunity to serve alongside some of the world's greatest leaders in both combat and peacetime. The U.S. military has long studied and trained leadership skills in the most critical of situations. While working with Julie McManus in similarly critical global corporate programs, I was most impressed with her strong capabilities and empathy. She stands among the very best. Her book, The Leadership Mirror reflects the same decisive, disciplined, and people-centered leadership I experienced firsthand working for her.

What sets Julie apart is her ability to lead with integrity while remaining agile and responsive to change. Julie understands that leadership is both mission and people. She earns trust through consistency, clear communication, and a deep respect for her team. She provides insight into those keen attributes in The Leadership Mirror. Leaders who want to create lasting change, not just short-term wins, will find this book both instructive and inspiring!"

— **Greg Vincent,**
Former U.S. Air Force Officer and
Organizational Leader

"Julie McManus brings uncommon clarity to leadership and change. In our work together, she helped leaders make sense of complexity, strengthen communication, and move change forward with intention. The Leadership Mirror captures that same ability to connect insight with execution.

This book challenges leaders to look inward and understand how their decisions, communication, and consistency shape culture and results. Julie offers practical guidance that supports leaders through the realities of change rather than theory."

— **Carrie Missele,**
Managing Partner, Project Violet

"In The Leadership Mirror, Julie McManus offers leaders a compassionate and unflinching invitation to return to themselves. Her work reminds us that sustainable leadership begins not with strategy but with self-awareness, not with control but with clarity, and not with performance but with presence. This book is a gift to anyone seeking to lead from a grounded, integrated place. Julie shows us how tending to the inner landscape transforms the outer one."

— **Lynnea Brinkerhoff,**
PCC, Organizational Advisor,
Executive Coach, and Whole-System
Transformation Practitioner

"What I appreciate most about The Leadership Mirror is its practicality. Julie McManus strips away the noise and gives leaders tools they can actually use. She challenges readers to be honest with themselves, understand what drives their behavior, and make small changes that create real impact. This book is a valuable companion for leaders who want to improve without the fluff."

— **Mary Beth Beaulieu,**
Organizational Development Professional

Foreword

Leadership gets talked about a lot—usually in terms of authority, position, or achievement. But the most effective leaders I've known would tell you something different: leadership starts long before the title. It starts with self-awareness, accountability, and the humility to keep growing.

I had the opportunity to work with Julie McManus early in her leadership journey while serving as Chairman of the Board at Proudfoot. She was still developing her leadership style then, but what stood out immediately was not showmanship. It was substance.

Julie was thoughtful in her approach. She took responsibility seriously. And she had the rare ability to receive feedback the right way—not defensively, not performatively, but as a genuine tool for growth. Over time, I watched that posture shape her into the kind of leader people trust: competent, steady, and consistent.

Julie understands a truth many leaders learn the hard way: leadership is not about control. It's about influence. It's not about projecting confidence. It's about building credibility. And it's not about saying the right things—it's about showing up the same way when no one is keeping score.

That is why *The Leadership Mirror* matters.

This book challenges leaders to slow down long enough to see themselves clearly—to examine assumptions, recognize patterns, and take responsibility for the impact they have on others. Julie does not offer slogans or quick fixes. She offers practical insight grounded in experience, reflection, and an honest understanding of the pressures leaders face.

The mirror metaphor is more than a clever idea. A mirror tells the truth. And leadership that lasts is always built on truth—about ourselves, about our blind spots, and about the culture we're creating by what we tolerate, reward, and model.

In a world that often rewards surface-level success, it takes discipline to lead from the inside out. It takes humility to keep learning. And it takes judgment to choose what is right over what is easy.

I believe *The Leadership Mirror* will serve leaders at many stages of their careers—from emerging leaders looking for traction to experienced leaders who want to regain clarity and lead with greater integrity. It calls leaders back to what is durable and trustworthy, and it provides a path to practice it.

Alan Steelman

#1 Best-selling author | Poet | Former Vice-Chairman Alexander Proudfoot | Former U.S. Congressman

TABLE OF CONTENTS

Introduction

Dear leader, aspiring leader, and reader who is not even sure they want to be called a leader anymore.

You picked up this book for a reason. Maybe you are sitting in your car after another long day, wondering how tomorrow could feel different. Maybe you are staring at your computer at nine at night, questioning whether this is what leadership is supposed to look like. Or maybe you are the one everyone believes has it all together, while you quietly ask yourself, "Am I actually any good at this?"

If any of that sounds familiar, you are in the right place. And you found this book at the exact time you needed it.

I know because I have spent four decades sitting with leaders just like you. Brilliant ones. Struggling ones. Many somewhere in between. From warehouse floors in Detroit to boardrooms in São Paulo, I have seen what leadership looks like when the pressure is real and the results matter.

I know you are tired. I know you are frustrated. I know there are moments you wonder if life was simpler when you were an individual contributor and your success was easier to measure. Whether you are just beginning your leadership journey, standing in the messy middle, or feeling completely burned out, this book is for you.

You do not have to figure it out alone. One of the biggest myths about leadership is that you are supposed to be the strongest person in the room. In reality, great leaders build communities of trust around them. They ask for help. They admit when they do not have all the answers. They find people who hold their confidence and remind them they do not have to carry everything by themselves.

Vulnerability in leadership is not weakness. It is the foundation of connection, safety, and loyalty. When you build that kind of trust, you stop leading from performance and start leading from partnership.

Here is something else I know. Good leaders question themselves. Bad leaders do not even realize something is off.

Leadership is one of the greatest responsibilities you will ever take on. It is hard, messy, and often exhausting. It will test you in ways you never expected. But when you get it right, when you see someone you have led step into their own greatness and begin lifting others, it is exhilarating. In that moment, when you realize you helped change someone's trajectory, you remember why leadership is worth it.

I truly believe most people do not wake up in the morning planning to struggle or fall short. They want to do a good job. They want to feel seen and valued. They want to be part of something bigger than themselves. I believe that with my whole heart. Yet something often happens between home and the workplace (even in remote work). For them, and maybe even you. The systems, processes, culture, pressure, customers, peers, and yes, leadership all shape how people show up. Over time the spark they began the day with can fade, and they find themselves repeating the same patterns day after day.

Not all of this is your responsibility to fix, but much of it is. Many organizations have figured out how to create conditions where people thrive. And this book aims to help you figure out your part in that work. Because when you understand your impact and lead with intention, everything around you begins to shift.

You have the ability to change the world around you. Maybe not in headline-making ways, but in real, lasting ways that matter to the people who show up every day hoping their leader genuinely cares.

So, the question becomes: are you ready to do something about where you are right now?

Why This Book?

Leadership was not something I learned from theory or books. The lessons came from years of guiding large-scale transformations, developing high-performing teams, and helping organizations rediscover their purpose. They came from sitting across from CEOs who had lost their spark and from supporting managers who were grieving the sudden loss of someone they trusted. They came from long days on warehouse floors with supervisors who held their teams together while everything around them was falling apart.

Those moments shaped my understanding of what leadership looks like when it truly counts, and they revealed why so many leaders lose themselves along the way.

My work has spanned industries, cultures, and challenges. I have led operational overhauls, cost-saving efforts, global leadership programs, and change initiatives that reshaped how people work together. I have coached executives through career-defining decisions. I have watched ordinary leaders do extraordinary things once they finally trusted themselves to lead differently.

Through all of it, one truth has remained. Leadership is not about having all the answers. It is about asking the right questions— starting with yourself.

The mirror I am talking about is not about vanity. It is about clarity. Just like you would not drive without checking your mirrors, you cannot lead effectively without regular self-reflection.

The mirror shows you three things.

- Who you really are, not who you think you are.

- How others experience your leadership, not how you intend to be experienced.

- What needs to shift for you to become the leader your team needs, not the leader you assume they want.

The lessons in this book come from those moments. The breakthroughs, the near misses, and the quiet repairs that happen when leaders stop performing leadership and start practicing it.

The Leadership Mirror is not another business book filled with recycled wisdom or surface-level motivation. It is a practical, field-tested guide built from real challenges, failures, and breakthroughs. I wrote it because too many capable leaders burn out, stall out, or walk away before they have ever truly seen themselves clearly. They chase expectations, perfection, and approval instead of purpose, clarity, and connection.

Whether you feel disconnected, uncertain, or simply curious about what comes next, this book will help you find your footing again. It is built on one simple truth: if you want to lead others better, you must start with yourself.

That is the work we will do together.

You will see that transformation is possible, even when you are tired, boxed in, or ready for something more. I will share the same tools and stories that have helped hundreds of leaders make that shift. What you discover, and how you apply it, is entirely up to you.

The mirror does not always show what we want to see. But if you are willing to look closely, it can reveal what has been missing, not to shame you, but to remind you who you can become.

So if you are ready to stop performing leadership and start practicing it, let us begin.

The mirror is waiting. And so is the leader you are capable of becoming.

Look inward. Lead outward.
Your journey starts now.

How to Use This Book

Throughout this book, you will find Tools and Mirror Moves designed to help you apply what you are learning in real time. These are not theoretical exercises. They are the same practices I use with the leaders I coach every day.

Here is what you can expect.

The Four Pillars of The Leadership Mirror Framework

Throughout this book you will follow a clear path that moves through the pillars of leadership: knowing yourself, managing your time and energy, shaping culture with intention, and expanding your influence and impact.

- Clarity of Self - Chapters 1 & 2

  You will learn to understand your strengths, values, beliefs, and purpose so you can lead from a place of truth rather than habit.

- Mastering Time & Energy – Chapter 3

  You will learn to master your priorities and manage your energy, not just your schedule, so you can lead with steadiness instead of depletion.

- Culture by Design – Chapter 4

  You will learn to shape the environment around you with intention and create the conditions where you and your teams can thrive.

- Expanding Influence and Impact – Chapters 5 – 9

You will learn to lead beyond yourself and create positive ripples that strengthen people, teams, and the culture around you.

Tools

The tools are not supplemental. They are the work.

Reading this book may increase your awareness. The tools will change your behavior.

Each tool appears exactly when you are ready to use it. Do not skip them. Do not "come back later" unless you actually schedule when later will be.

Every tool has a corresponding worksheet designed to slow you down and force clarity. Insight fades quickly. Written reflection anchors it.

If you want different results, you must interrupt old patterns. The tools are how you do that.

Mirror Moves

After every tool, you will find a Mirror Move.

The tool creates awareness.

The Mirror Move turns awareness into action.

Writing something down is not transformation. Acting on it is.

These Mirror Moves are not motivational prompts. They are real-world applications designed to move you beyond reflection and into behavior.

They are intentionally simple and intentionally uncomfortable.

They may ask you to:

- Start the conversation you have been avoiding.
- Set the boundary you keep postponing.
- Ask for feedback you may not enjoy hearing.
- Make a decision aligned with your values instead of your fear.

This is where leadership actually shifts.

Insight without action becomes intellectual entertainment. Action, even small action, creates momentum.

Do not rush past these. Choose one Mirror Move. Schedule it. Execute it. Then observe what changes in you and around you.

Leadership grows when you stretch beyond what feels automatic.

If you skip the Mirror Move, you may skip the growth.

Do I Really Need to Read the Whole Book?

I would love it if you did.

But I also know you might be in a hurry. Maybe you are facing a specific challenge, need clarity quickly, or simply do not have the time to read nine chapters before something in your world demands action.

You picked up this book because something is not working the way you want it to. You want focus, direction, and the fastest path to impact.

While the full journey will serve you, the most important thing is to start where you are, not where you think you should be. Use the quick assessment below to find your starting point and identify which chapters will help you most right now.

Quick Leadership Assessment

Find Your Starting Point

Rate each statement on a scale of 1-5 (1=never, 5=always):
- I feel clear about my values and how they show up in my leadership
- I manage my energy and time intentionally rather than reactively
- My team feels safe to bring me problems and honest feedback
- I handle conflict and difficult conversations with confidence
- When things go wrong, I focus on learning rather than blame
- People seek me out for advice and guidance
- I consistently develop others and help them grow
- I make decisions that align with my long-term vision
- I bounce back quickly from setbacks and failures
- I feel energized by my leadership role most days

SCORING:

35-50: You're ready for advanced influence work (Peruse Chapter one and then move to Chapters 5-7)

20-34: You have solid foundations but need focused growth (Start with Chapter 1, focus on Chapters 3-5)

10-19: You're in crisis or burnout mode (Start with Chapters 1-3, then 6)

I know we all love an assessment; however, you may want to look at things a little differently. Look at the paths below. Maybe that works better for you. Determine which path you are on and focus on those chapters first.

Reader Pathways

THE CRISIS PATH	THE GROWTH PATH	THE ACCELERATION PATH
(For leaders who are struggling/overwhelmed)	(For leaders ready to level up)	(For strong leaders wanting maximum impact)
"If you're barely keeping your head above water, feeling like you're failing, or your team has lost confidence in you:"	"If you're doing okay but know you could be more effective and influential:"	"If you're already a solid leader but want to become exceptional:"
▶ Start with Chapter 1 (The Mirror) - You need clarity first.	▶ Start with Chapter 1 (The Mirror) - Deepen your self-awareness.	▶ Skim Chapter 1 for any blind spots
▶ Move to Chapter 2 (Managing Your Inner World) - Get your mental game stable.	▶ Focus on Chapters 4-5 (Culture and Influence) - Expand your impact.	▶ Use Chapter 3 (Time/Energy) as needed for optimization.
▶ Then move to Chapter 6 (When the Mirror Cracks) - Learn to lead through the hard stuff.	▶ Use Chapter 3 (Time/Energy) as needed for optimization.	▶ Dive deep into Chapters 5, 7, and 8 (Influence, Legacy, Impact)
	▶ End with Chapters 7-9 for long-term vision.	▶ Use other chapters as diagnostic tools when you hit obstacles.

Chapter Roadmap

- Chapter 1: THE MIRROR → Self-awareness and honest assessment

- Chapter 2: INNER WORLD → Mental and emotional management

- Chapter 3: TIME & ENERGY → Sustainable leadership practices

- Chapter 4: CULTURE → Intentional environment design

- Chapter 5: INFLUENCE → Building authentic leadership impact

- Chapter 6: WHEN IT CRACKS → Leading through failure and crisis

- Chapter 7: LEGACY → Living your values daily

- Chapter 8: EXPANDED IMPACT → Leveraging growth for bigger results

- Chapter 9: LIFELONG JOURNEY → Making it sustainable

While I'd love for you to dive into the entire book, please meet yourself where you are and dive in where it makes the most sense.

When the urgency settles and you have the space, come back and read the entire book. Each chapter builds on the next and will strengthen you in ways that matter long-term.

CHAPTER ONE

The Mirror – Leadership Starts With You

What do you see when you look in the mirror?

No, really. Stop reading for a moment.

If you're at home, go find a mirror. If you're reading this on a plane, in a coffee shop, or somewhere public, pull out your phone and switch to the front-facing camera.

Look at yourself for thirty seconds. Not a glance. Not a quick check of your appearance. Really look.

What do you see?

Not the polished version of yourself that shows up in your profile picture, or the confident one who walks into meetings armed with talking points. I mean the real you. The version that surfaces when no one is watching. The one who flinches when your leadership gets questioned. The one who stiffens when your authority feels undermined.

That's where we begin. Because you cannot lead anyone else until you are honest with yourself.

This chapter begins the first pillar of The Leadership Mirror Framework, Clarity of Self, where you learn to understand who you are as a leader before you try to influence anyone else.

Leadership doesn't start with a strategy or a new team charter. It starts with self-awareness. It begins with the courage to sit with what is true about you: your values, your blind spots, and your patterns under stress. It takes courage to ask, "What is it like to be led by me?" and to truly listen to the answer.

Why Looking Inward Feels Hard

Looking inward is not easy work. You have spent years building credibility, influence, and confidence. Questioning what might be underneath the surface can feel risky. But self-awareness is not about self-doubt. It is about accuracy.

When you see yourself clearly, you make better decisions. You lead with intention. You repair faster when you get it wrong. The challenge is that most leaders want to skip this part and move quickly to the "how" of leadership. But if you ignore the mirror, everything that follows rests on shaky ground. Real leadership begins when you are willing to look, even when you do not love what you see.

And let's be honest. This kind of reflection is uncomfortable for a reason.

Your brain is wired to protect you from threat, and honest self-examination can feel threatening. It asks you to question the stories you tell yourself, the habits you defend, and the identity you have worked hard to build. Your survival brain does not know the difference between real danger and feedback that makes you feel exposed. It reacts to both with the same instinct: look away.

That resistance is not a flaw. It is human nature.

In my work with leaders, I have noticed a pattern. The stronger the resistance, the more important the insight on the other side. Your brain does not resist what is trivial. It resists what matters.

So if you feel a tightening in your chest right now, if part of you wants to skip ahead to the "practical" chapters, congratulations. You have just found your growth edge. That discomfort is not a sign that you are doing it wrong. It is the first sign that you are doing it right.

What You Notice When You Look Clearly

Here's what will happen: at some point in this process, you're going to see something in the mirror that makes you uncomfortable. Maybe you'll realize you're micromanaging more than you thought. Maybe you'll see that your "high standards" sometimes come across as harsh criticism. Maybe you'll discover that your need to be liked is preventing you from having necessary difficult conversations.

When this happens, resist these common temptations:

- Don't Look Away: The urge will be to dismiss what you see, rationalize it, or blame others. "My team just needs more structure." "I wouldn't have to micromanage if they were more reliable." "The culture here doesn't support direct feedback." Stay with what you see.

- Get Curious, Not Critical: Instead of asking "What's wrong with me?" ask "How did this pattern develop?" and "What was this behavior trying to protect or achieve?" Most leadership patterns developed for good reasons. Understanding the why helps you change more effectively.

- Start Small: Don't try to overhaul your entire leadership style overnight. Pick one specific behavior or pattern to work on. Master that change before moving to the next one.

- Get Support: Find someone who can help you see your blind spots with compassion. This might be a coach, a trusted peer, or a mentor. Change is hard to do alone.

The mirror isn't meant to shame you. It's meant to free you.

How Leaders Avoid What They See

Sarah was a VP who almost walked out of my workshop on day one.

"I don't have time for self-reflection," she announced during our first break. "I have a business to run. I came here for strategies, not therapy."

I asked her one question: "How's that working out for you?"

She started listing her achievements—revenue growth, successful product launches, industry recognition. Then she paused.

"But my second director just quit," she admitted. "My team says I'm impossible to please. And honestly? I haven't enjoyed work in two years."

"So, you have all the strategies," I said. "But something's still not working."

Sarah stayed for the workshop. The mirror showed her something she hadn't expected: she was leading from fear. Fear of failure, fear of being seen as weak, fear of not being enough. That fear made her demanding, critical, and impossible to satisfy—including herself.

Six months later, she sent me a note: "Still running a business. But now I'm also leading people. Turns out that's what I was missing."

That's what the mirror does. It gives you back the part of leadership that control took away

My Own Moment in the Mirror

I didn't always like what I saw in my mirror.

For years, I led with intensity. I set high standards, pushed for performance, and prided myself on being strong, steady, and unshakable. I believed emotions didn't belong in the workplace. Leadership, I thought, meant control, having the answers, and keeping things on track no matter the cost.

To be fair, it worked. The team delivered. We hit goals, met deadlines, and produced results. But underneath, tension simmered. Relationships were strained. I was exhausted, and so was everyone else. Burnout didn't arrive suddenly. It built quietly until it could no longer be ignored.

My intensity showed up in ways I didn't see. I jumped into problems before fully understanding them. I cut off discussions once I thought I knew the answer. I gave feedback that was accurate but landed as criticism. When people brought me concerns, I skipped over feelings and went straight to fixing.

Then came a turning point. One of my most respected team members asked to talk. Nervously, she said, "I know you care about the work and about us getting results. But sometimes it feels like you don't care about us as people."

That hit me hard. Because I did care. Deeply. But my leadership style wasn't communicating that.

It was the moment I stopped asking, "what's wrong with them?" and started asking, *what is it like to be led by me?*

That question changed everything. I began noticing how often I interrupted, how tightly I held control, and how my good intentions were landing as pressure. I wasn't trying to be difficult. I was trying to be competent. But my version of competence was creating disconnection.

So, I started to lead differently. I listened more than I talked. I asked questions before giving answers. I acknowledged emotions in the room before solving problems. I apologized when I got it wrong. And something remarkable happened. The work got better. The relationships grew stronger. The team became more self-sufficient.

I didn't lose authority. I gained trust.

The Patterns You Carry

Every leader brings invisible baggage into the role. Past experiences, inherited beliefs, cultural messages, and old wounds that shape how you lead, often without your knowledge.

These influences don't announce themselves. They show up in the moment when pressure hits. In how you react when someone challenges your decision in a meeting. In what happens inside you when a team member starts crying during a one-on-one. In the automatic response you have when someone questions your authority.

When you've been trained to suppress emotions, you don't just suppress your own. You suppress the entire emotional reality of your workplace. This creates infinite challenges for both you and your team.

People stop bringing you their real concerns because they know you're not comfortable with anything that isn't purely logical. They learn to package their frustrations as "process issues" instead of telling you they're overwhelmed. They edit themselves before they speak to you, filtering out anything that might seem too passionate or personal.

You end up leading a team of people who are "performing" emotions rather than experiencing them. Professional. Composed.

Detached. And ultimately less creative, less engaged, and less honest with you about what's really happening.

The irony is that while you think you're keeping things efficient and focused, you're creating more problems. Because emotions don't disappear when you ignore them. They go underground. They show up as aggression, decreased performance, quiet quitting, or people suddenly leaving for "better opportunities."

The Authenticity Advantage

Here's what most leaders don't realize: your team already knows you're human. They can feel when you're frustrated, stressed, excited, or worried, even when you think you're hiding it. The difference is whether you acknowledge that reality or pretend it doesn't exist.

When you give yourself permission to be more real, not dramatically or unprofessionally, but genuinely, something shifts. People start trusting you more because they can see you. They stop walking on eggshells because they know where you stand. They bring you better information because they're not spending energy managing your emotional reactions.

This doesn't mean you become an emotional free-for-all. It means you stop treating human feelings like a problem to be solved and start treating them like information to be considered.

Other Baggage You Might Be Carrying

Emotional suppression is just one example. You might also be carrying:

The belief that you must have all the answers, so you never say "I don't know" even when you don't. The message that asking for help is weakness, so you struggle alone instead of leveraging your team's expertise. The idea that leadership means being in control of everything, so you micromanage instead of empowering others.

Maybe you learned that showing uncertainty makes people lose confidence in you, so you project false confidence even when you're genuinely unsure. Maybe you picked up the idea that you can't be both liked and respected, so you choose distance over connection.

All these invisible influences shape how you show up as a leader. And until you become aware of them, they're making choices for you.

The Emotional Labor No One Talks About

There is a kind of work in leadership that never appears on org charts or performance reviews, but it shapes every decision, every conversation, and every outcome. It is the emotional labor of leadership.

It is the quiet work of carrying unspoken tension. The weight of being the person others turn to with their concerns, even when no one asks how you are doing. The self-control required to stay steady under pressure. The courage it takes to walk into a room and say, "We got it wrong," even when your own heart feels heavy.

This labor is invisible, but it is real. And it can be exhausting.

No one prepares you for the energy it takes to hold space for others when your own reserves are low. No one explains how isolating it can feel to be the person everyone depends on for calm, direction, or hope.

During a massive reorganization earlier in my career, this reality became impossible to ignore. People were scared about their jobs. Morale was collapsing. Every day someone showed up with fear, frustration, or anger about the uncertainty ahead. I listened. I empathized. I offered whatever reassurance I could.

What they did not know was that I was scared too. The answers they wanted were the same answers I wished someone would give me. So, the fear stayed private, while I carried everyone else's emotional weight on top of my own. At the end of the day, the exhaustion came not from the tasks, but from the emotional energy required to stay steady for everyone else.

That season taught me something essential about emotional labor: you cannot pour from an empty cup. Without tending to your own emotional needs, there is nothing left to give.

So, I learned to process my emotions outside of work. I asked for support instead of always being the one offering it. I became more honest with my team about the challenges we were facing, without pretending I had everything under control.

And something surprising happened. Their confidence did not fade. Their connection deepened. They trusted me more, not less, because they could see the human being behind the role.

Emotional labor is not weakness. It is part of leading with heart.

If you have ever ended a day completely drained from simply holding everything together, you are not alone. And you are not doing it wrong. You are doing the real work. This kind of leadership may not always be recognized, but it is always felt.

From Managing to Leading

Most of us were trained to manage. You manage deadlines, budgets, schedules, and problems. You keep things moving and in order. That's what gets rewarded.

But if you're feeling disconnected from your work, it might be because you're managing when you need to be leading.

Management is about control. Leadership is about connection. Management focuses on what needs to get done. Leadership asks who you need to be while doing it.

You can't manage your way into loving this work again. Control might keep things moving, but connection is what moves people. And connection starts with knowing yourself well enough to show up intentionally.

When there's a gap between who you are and how you're leading, your people feel it. They might not be able to name it, but they know something's off. And so do you.

That disconnect you're feeling. It often comes from leading out of habit instead of purpose. From reacting instead of responding. From avoiding the hard conversations or bulldozing through them.

Self-Awareness Isn't Optional - It's Essential

Let's clear something up. Self-awareness is not a bonus feature for leaders. It's not a luxury. It's a survival skill.

When you're not aware of your inner world, you:

- React instead of respond.

- Avoid hard conversations or bulldoze through them.

- Make assumptions that go unchallenged.

- Lead from fear or ego instead of purpose and principle

- Create unintended consequences that you then have to clean up.

The most dangerous leaders I've encountered weren't malicious. (Well, maybe a few of them were.) They were unaware. They had blind spots the size of billboards, and no one felt safe enough to name them. That kind of leadership creates confusion, resentment, and disconnection.

Don't be that leader.

Your Job Isn't to Be Someone Else

Leadership is about becoming more of who you are on purpose, with self-awareness and intention.

When you lead from that place, everything starts to align:

- Your team trusts you because they know what to expect.
- You trust yourself because you're not pretending.
- You build a culture of honesty, accountability, and care.
- You make decisions from a place of clarity rather than reaction.
- You handle pressure better because you understand your own patterns.
- You build stronger relationships because people experience you as genuine.

This isn't a magic fix. But it is a powerful shift. One that will change how you lead and how you feel about leading.

Reflection Isn't Luxury. It's Discipline.

One of the stories we tell ourselves in leadership is that real leaders are too busy for reflection, self-care, or self-love.

The reality is, if you don't have time to reflect, you don't have time to lead.

Reflection is where your insight lives. It's how patterns come into view. It's how growth becomes possible. And it doesn't require a sabbatical or a mountaintop.

It requires a pause. A question. A willingness to look inward. That's not fluff. That's strategy. That's leadership.

Your Turn in the Mirror: Tools to Get Started

You're not just here to read. You're here to do the work. Here are the tools to help you really connect with the concepts in this first chapter. Yes, this will require more time and effort, however they will help you to assimilate the concepts more quickly. Practice makes perfect they say… so give it a go. You have nothing to lose and everything to gain.

Tool 1: Mirror Exercise: Your Starting Point

Purpose: To Notice your starting point as a leader. This isn't about judging yourself. It's about seeing yourself.

Part A: The Private Mirror (What you see)

- When I'm under extreme pressure, I tend to...

- The leadership behavior I hide from others is...

- If my team could change one thing about how I lead, they'd probably say...

- The last time I received feedback that stung, it was about...

- I know I should stop... but I keep doing it anyway.

Part B: The Public Mirror (What others see)

- My team would describe my leadership style as...

- When I walk into a room, the energy typically...

- People come to me when they need...
- People avoid me when...
- My reputation as a leader is probably...

Part C: The Gap (Where growth lives) Look at your answers above. Where do you see the biggest disconnect between:

- Who you think you are and how you actually behave?
- What you intend and what others experience?
- The leader you want to be and the leader you are today?

Pick ONE gap you identified. Just one. Write it on a sticky note and put it somewhere you'll see it daily. This is your mirror work for the next week. You aren't going to fix everything at once. Just watch this one pattern with curiosity and adjust your behavior as you see fit.

Example: "I think I'm approachable, but my team avoids bringing me problems."

Mirror Move: Pick the one area that stings the most. The one you rated lowest. The one you wanted to skip past. That's the one you may need to focus on first.

Ask yourself:

- What's really driving this score?
- What's one honest conversation I've been avoiding around this?
- Who could give me unfiltered feedback about how I'm showing up here?

Then, act. Pick one small, uncomfortable step that would move the needle in this area and do it this week. It might be asking a peer for feedback. Apologizing. Delegating. Saying "No". Speaking up.

Leadership is about doing the work where it matters.

Tool 2: The Leadership Blind Spot Identifier

Purpose: Help leaders discover what they can't see about themselves.

Instructions:

1. Ask three people (one direct report, one peer, one superior) this exact question: "What's one thing I do as a leader that I might not realize I'm doing?"

2. Listen without defending or explaining.

3. Thank them for their honesty.

4. Look for patterns across the three responses.

5. Identify one blind spot to work on this month.

Mirror Move: Share what you learned with your team. Say something like: "I asked for some feedback about my leadership blind spots. Here's what I learned, and here's what I'm going to work on." This vulnerability builds trust and gives your team permission to be honest with you going forward.

Tool 3: The Values Clarifier - What Do I Stand For?

Purpose: To name your personal leadership values and check if you're living them.

Instructions: Write down your top 3-5 values. Then for each, answer:

- Where in my leadership am I honoring this value?

- Where am I compromising it?

- What's one action I can take this week to realign?

Mirror Move: Values aren't just meant to be named; they are meant to be visible.

Choose one value you're compromising. Then take one bold step to realign, publicly.

Maybe it's having a hard conversation you've been avoiding. Admitting a mistake. Shifting your time, not just your talk. Saying no to something that's out of alignment. Saying yes to something that scares you and fits who you want to be.

Then, ask someone you trust: "Do you see this value in how I lead?" Be ready for what they say. Growth lives in their answer.

A value is a core belief or principle that guides how you think, act, and make decisions. It's what matters most to you, deep down, especially when no one's watching.

Values are not goals or traits. They're not what you want to have, they're what you stand for.

In leadership, your values shape:

- How you lead under pressure

- What you prioritize and protect

- What lines you won't cross

- How others experience you

For example:

- If you value integrity, you'll speak the truth even when it's uncomfortable.

- If you value growth, you'll seek feedback and challenge the status quo.

- If you value belonging, you'll create space where others feel seen and safe.

The problem? Many leaders say they value things, but don't lead in a way that reflects them. That's why identifying and aligning with your real values isn't fluffy work, it's foundational.

Tool 4: Triggers and Triumphs

Purpose: To notice the emotional patterns that drive your leadership for better or worse.

Instructions: List 3 situations where you felt triggered or reactive.

- What happened? How did you respond?
- What belief or fear got activated?
- What could you do differently next time?
- What impact did your reaction have on others and on the outcome?

Then flip it: List 3 leadership wins or "triumphs."

What made those moments possible? What strengths did you lean into?

How can you build on them?

Mirror Move: Patterns don't change through insight alone. They change through practice.

This week, choose one emotional trigger you uncovered and set an intention to respond differently the next time it shows up.

Before a tough meeting or conversation, pause and ask yourself: "What story am I telling myself?" "What's really driving this reaction?"

Then choose your response on purpose, not out of fear, ego, or habit.

Ask a trusted peer or coach to help you spot that old pattern in real time. Give them permission to call it out.

Because self-awareness is good. Shared awareness? That's where transformation happens.

Final Thoughts: Looking Inward Before Leading Outward

This is where your leadership journey really begins. Not with a new strategy or skill, but with the courage to see yourself clearly.

Everything else in this book builds on what happens in this chapter. Clarity of Self is the foundation. Once you begin seeing yourself accurately, you are ready for the next part of the framework, where we deepen this pillar and begin connecting your self-awareness to your purpose and leadership identity.

Every tool, every technique, every transformation starts with your willingness to look in the mirror and stay there long enough to see what needs to shift.

The mirror isn't always kind. But it is honest. And that honesty is the foundation of every great leader I've ever known.

Your team is counting on you to do this work. Not because they need you to be perfect, but because they need you to be real. They need a leader who knows themselves well enough to lead with intention rather than reaction, purpose rather than fear, authenticity rather than performance.

Before you turn to Chapter 2, go back to that mirror one more time. Look yourself in the eyes and make a commitment: "I'm willing to see myself clearly, even when it's uncomfortable. I'm willing to grow, even when it's hard. I'm willing to become the leader my team deserves."

Then ask yourself two final questions:

What is it like to be led by me? And, am I proud of the answer?

CHAPTER TWO

Managing Your Inner World

Before you can lead a team, you have to learn to lead yourself- your thoughts, your emotions, and your energy.

If you're tempted to skip the mirror work, consider this: managing your inner world becomes much clearer when you've first seen yourself honestly. This chapter continues the first pillar of The Leadership Mirror Framework, Clarity of Self, where you deepen your understanding of who you are as a leader. Clarity becomes the anchor for every leadership choice you make.

Here's what many stuck leaders don't realize: the reason leadership feels so draining isn't the work itself. It's all the invisible ways your mental and emotional energy is leaking out without you noticing. And those leaks? They all start with the patterns you saw (or refused to see) in the mirror.

But seeing yourself clearly is only the first step. Now we need to talk about what happens next: managing what you discovered.

Your inner world, the voice in your head, the story you tell yourself, and the way you respond to pressure, shape your leadership far more than any strategy, tool, or certification ever will. And when it's chaotic, everything else becomes harder.

What happens inside you eventually shows up outside you.

Where Your Energy Really Goes

Let's start with something concrete. Think about yesterday. By 3 PM, were you energized or exhausted?

If you're like many leaders, you might be running on fumes. Some leaders hit their stride in the afternoon. Others feel like their tank is empty by then. The key is knowing which one you are. Part of looking in the mirror is noticing how your energy rises and falls throughout the day. When do you feel sharp and focused? When do you need fifteen minutes to stop and breathe? What tasks fit best in those different zones?

Now think about where your energy actually went yesterday. Sure, you had meetings. You made decisions. You put out fires. But I'm talking about the invisible energy drains that no one tracks.

Perhaps it went to:

- The Replay Drain: That awkward comment from Tuesday's meeting that you've replayed seventeen times, each time crafting the perfect response you didn't say.

- The Translation Drain: Wondering what your boss really meant when they said your presentation was "interesting." You've assigned twelve different meanings to that word, none of them good.

- The Avoidance Drain: The feedback conversation you've been postponing for three weeks. It's taking more energy to avoid it than it would take to have it.

- The Catastrophizing Drain: Running worst-case scenarios about the project that's behind schedule. You've mentally lived through getting fired twice today, and it's only 10 AM.

- The Context-Switching Drain: Trying to remember if you responded to that important email while simultaneously planning tomorrow's presentation while half-listening to the current meeting.

You may be experiencing all five of these right now, plus a few others I haven't named.

These aren't time management problems. These are mental load problems. And they're exhausting you more than your actual work.

Most leaders spend more energy thinking about their work than doing it. And that's where we're going to start.

The Battle in Your Brain

Leadership is as much a mental game as it is a relational or strategic one. Your brain, brilliant as it is, isn't always working in your favor.

Most of us are walking around with brains wired for survival, not success. We are constantly scanning for threats, replaying mistakes, and assuming the worst. It is not a personal flaw. It is biology.

Neuroscience shows that when the brain senses danger, even something as small as a tense meeting or a difficult conversation, the amygdala triggers a stress response that narrows our thinking and heightens emotion. Dr. Daniel Goleman, author of *Emotional Intelligence*, explains that "when the amygdala hijacks the brain, it floods us with stress hormones that make rational thought almost impossible."

This isn't just theory. Research by Dr. Rick Hanson, author of "Hardwiring Happiness," shows our brains have what he calls a "negativity bias." We're literally wired like Velcro for negative experiences and Teflon for positive ones. Hanson's studies found that it takes five positive interactions to offset one negative one. That's why that awkward comment from Tuesday's meeting stays with you while the three compliments you received that day disappear.

When we lead from that state of fear, scarcity, or defense, we protect instead of create. We react instead of reflect. Over time, it keeps us stuck in survival mode and drains the energy our teams need most.

I once worked with a leader named Dominique. In one of our early conversations, she said, "If it weren't for my employees, my job would be easy."

I paused. I'm thinking... *your employees ARE your job.*

Instead of reacting, I got curious. "Tell me more," I said. "What makes you feel that way?"

She went on to describe how her team consistently delivered sub-par work. She felt like she was constantly correcting mistakes, redoing tasks, or cleaning up messes. It was exhausting.

So, we took a closer look. I asked her to walk me through a recent deliverable that had missed the mark.

"Well," she said, "David submitted a document that left out key details and was full of formatting issues. It wasn't polished, and it didn't reflect well on me."

"What were the expectations you gave him?" I asked.

Silence.

Finally, she admitted that she had dashed off a vague email with a quick request and no real context, no explanation of the audience, the purpose, or the standards she was expecting. And regarding David's formatting issues? She never set the expectation of what she wanted. She would regularly fix the issues herself.

That moment was a turning point. Mainly because it wasn't the first time. Dominique realized her frustration wasn't just about her team. It was about the assumptions and stories she was telling herself, stories like "They should just know", "They're not capable", or "It's faster if I do it myself."

Underneath those stories was a quiet belief that she was the only one who could do things right. Her need for control was disguised as high standards, and it was costing her team their confidence and growth.

Her inner narrative was shaping her leadership behavior. And it was creating the very outcomes she feared.

This is how it works: Your thoughts drive your emotions. Your emotions drive your behavior. Your behavior creates your results.

If your inner world is full of blame, self-doubt, resentment, or anxiety, then guess what your team is picking up on? But when your internal dialogue is grounded in clarity, curiosity, and care, people feel that too. They lean in. They respond. They grow.

The Stories We Tell Ourselves

Before we dive into solutions, let's name what's really happening. We're all walking around with stories in our heads. Stories about ourselves, our teams, our capabilities, our worth.

Most of these stories were written years ago, maybe decades ago. Some helpful parents, teachers, or boss planted a seed: "You're not good at public speaking." "You're too sensitive for leadership." "Real leaders don't show emotion." "You have to work twice as hard to get half the credit."

These stories become our internal soundtrack. And here's the problem: we rarely question them. We just live them.

Dr. Carol Dweck's research on mindset reveals just how powerful these internal narratives are. In her studies at Stanford, she found that leaders with a "fixed mindset" (believing abilities are static) created cultures 45% less likely to innovate compared to leaders with a "growth mindset" (believing abilities can develop). The story in your head literally shapes the culture around you.

Marcus was a client of mine who ran a small but growing distribution company. He was bright. His team respected him. The business was thriving. But Marcus was miserable.

"I feel like I'm waiting for someone to figure out I don't know what I'm doing," he told me in our first session.

When we dug deeper, we found the story underneath: "I'm just the kid from the wrong side of town who got lucky. I don't belong here."

That story was written when Marcus was twelve years old, sitting in a scholarship interview for a private school, feeling like everyone could see he didn't fit in. It had been running his leadership for fifteen years.

The story wasn't true anymore. Maybe it never was. But it shaped every decision he made. How he presented in meetings, whether he spoke up with bold ideas, how he positioned himself for growth opportunities.

Six months later, Marcus sent me a short email that said everything: "Stopped trying to be the leader my dad wanted me to be. Started being the leader my team needed me to be. Best quarter we've ever had. And for the first time in five years, I actually enjoy Monday mornings."

That's what happens when you stop performing someone else's version of leadership and start practicing your own. The external results follow the internal shift. Always.

Marcus still runs a successful company. But now he runs it as himself, not as an impersonation of his father. His team meetings have energy. People challenge ideas. They laugh. And yes, they still deliver results. Better results because people want to work for a leader who is real.

Your stories are doing the same thing. What story do you tell yourself when things go wrong? When you make a mistake? When someone challenges your authority? When you're facing something new?

Those stories aren't neutral. They're either fueling your leadership or sabotaging it.

From Inner Critic to Inner Coach

Neuroscientist Dr. Ethan Kross found that how we talk to ourselves matters as much as what we say. His research shows that using your own name when self-talking (saying "Julie, you can handle this" instead of "I can handle this") creates psychological distance that reduces anxiety by 50% and improves performance under pressure. It's the difference between being trapped in the problem and being able to observe it.

Every leader I've ever coached has an inner critic. And often, the more successful they are, the louder that critic becomes.

You know the voice:

"You're not ready for this."

"They're going to see right through you."

"Why can't you just get it right?"

"You're too much. Or not enough."

That voice might sound familiar. But don't mistake it for truth. It's just programming. Old, outdated, often inherited from childhood, early career experiences, or a harsh boss. That voice developed to protect you, and now it's just holding you back.

The alternative? You need to turn down the inner critic and turn up your inner coach.

Your inner coach doesn't sugarcoat or make excuses. But it does speak with wisdom and compassion. It asks better questions:

- "What do I know is true right now?"

- "What else might be going on here?"

- "What would the leader I aspire to be do next?"

Melanie was a high-performing director who was exhausted and questioning whether leadership was worth it. She constantly second-guessed herself, replayed conversations in her head, and felt like she was one misstep away from being found out.

Her inner critic had built her career by ensuring that she was always hard on herself. Every success came with a whisper: "You could've done better. Don't get too comfortable. Don't let them see you struggle."

We began by naming that voice. She called it *The Taskmaster.* It had helped her climb the ladder but left her worn out from the climb.

Through our coaching, Melanie began to develop a new inner voice she called *Grace.* Grace did not scold or shame her. She asked better questions. Instead of *What's wrong with me?* she asked, *What can I learn from this?* Instead of *You're falling behind,* she reminded Melanie, *You're finding your rhythm.*

The shift wasn't instant, but it was real. Within a few months, she was taking more risks and feeling less anxious. She delegated more, trusted her team, and started receiving feedback that she was more present and easier to approach. Her performance improved, and so did her team's.

That's the power of replacing the inner critic with an inner coach. It doesn't make you soft, it makes you sustainable.

The Hidden Energy Drains Nobody Talks About

Here's where most leadership advice falls short, it focuses on what you do without addressing what's depleting you. The biggest energy drains aren't in your calendar. They are in your head.

This includes every unresolved conflict you're avoiding. Every decision you've been putting off. Every conversation you need to have but haven't. Every commitment you made but can't remember. Even, every email sitting in your inbox that makes you feel slightly guilty when you see it.

This mental clutter doesn't just live in your head. It shows up in your leadership:

- Decision-making Impact: You postpone difficult conversations until they become crises.

- You say "yes" to requests without considering your actual capacity.

- You make the same decision multiple times because you can't remember what you have already decided.

- You rarely say "no" to things you have no desire nor bandwidth to do.

- Communication Breakdown: You interrupt people mid-sentence because your brain is already jumping to the next thing.

- You send unclear emails because you're rushing to clear your mental inbox.

- You forget what you promised people in previous conversations.

- Team and Relationship Effects: You delegate tasks but then redo them yourself because explaining feels harder than doing.

- You become impatient with questions you feel you've already answered.

- You withdraw from informal conversations because small talk feels like mental noise.

- Strategic and Vision Issues: You focus on urgent emails instead of important long-term planning.

- You attend meetings without preparing because preparation feels like another task.

- You lose sight of bigger goals because you're managing too many moving pieces.

- Personal Energy Drains: You work late trying to catch up on the thinking you couldn't do during the day.

- You feel guilty about things you've forgotten rather than systems you haven't created.

- You bring work stress home because your brain won't turn off the mental checklist.

I worked with a CEO who was constantly exhausted. She was working 70-hour weeks and still felt behind. When we mapped out where her mental energy was going, we discovered something shocking: she was spending 2-3 hours a day thinking about one difficult employee.

Not managing the employee. Not developing a plan. Just thinking. Worrying. Replaying conversations. Imagining scenarios.

That mental loop was costing her more than the employee's actual performance issues.

Emotions Are Data, Not Directives

Suppressing your emotions doesn't make you stronger. It makes you unpredictable, reactive, and disconnected. What makes a leader powerful is the ability to feel emotion, understand it, and choose how to respond with intention.

Years ago, I had a heated argument (AKA screaming match) with my boss. Right in the middle of the office. In front of everyone.

The team had been under pressure for weeks. We had tight deadlines, long hours, the kind of stress that eats at morale. Then my boss made a last-minute decision that would undo much of the team's work. I was furious.

And instead of taking a breath or pulling him aside, I let my anger take the wheel. We went toe-to-toe in front of the entire team, raised voices, tense jaws, locked stares.

I thought I was being strong. I thought I was standing up for my team. What I was doing was reacting without intention. I was letting my emotions drive, without a map.

Later, I realized something important: My emotions weren't a problem. My lack of regulation was.

The anger came from a place of care and loyalty, but my delivery short-circuited any real influence. I didn't pause. I didn't reflect. I just reacted.

That moment taught me what I now teach others: Emotions are data. Not directives.

They tell us what matters. But we get to choose what to do with that information. When you build emotional fluency, you can easily notice the signs: your body tightening, your tone sharpening, and your thoughts racing. This understanding allows you to create just enough space to shift.

The Ripple Effect of Your Inner World

Your mood is contagious.

That might make you uncomfortable, but it's an important truth.

Whatever you're feeling and thinking, your team picks up on. Even when you think you're hiding it well. When you walk into a room stressed, your team feels it. When you're checked out mentally, they sense it. When you're confident and grounded, they feel that too.

I once worked with a leadership team where the CEO was going through a difficult divorce. He was trying to keep his personal life separate from work, but his emotional state bled into every meeting. The team became tense, cautious, and less creative. Productivity dropped.

It wasn't until he acknowledged what was happening and got support for managing his emotional state that the team culture began to shift.

Your inner world isn't just personal. It's professional. It affects everyone around you.

You Can't Control Everything, But You Can Control You

You don't get to control everything. Not how people interpret your words. Not whether your colleague shows up in a bad mood. Not the market. Or your boss. Or your team's Wi-Fi connection.

But here's what you can control: your breath, your preparation, your internal narrative, and your presence in the room.

Here's what I want you to understand: when you do this inner work, you're not just changing yourself. You're changing your entire leadership ecosystem.

When you manage your inner world well:

- Your team feels safer taking risks and sharing ideas.

- Difficult conversations become more productive.
- Your decision-making improves because you're not operating from fear or reactivity
- You model emotional intelligence for your organization.
- You create space for others to be authentic too.
- Your stress decreases and your energy increases.
- You become the leader who people want to follow.

By strengthening the soft skills of inner work you become a more effective leader.

Your Turn: Tools to Manage Your Inner World

These tools will help you get inside your own head and clean up the clutter.

Tool 5: Daily Reset Tracker

Purpose: To help you tune into your thoughts, emotions, and energy so you can reset instead of reacting.

Instructions: Each day, take 5 minutes to reflect:

- What thought dominated my day today?
- How did that thought impact my mood or behavior?
- What drained my energy?
- What restored it?
- What's one thing I can shift tomorrow?

You'll start noticing patterns. And those patterns? That's where change begins.

Mirror Move: Patterns are powerful, but sharing them? That's where transformation accelerates.

At the end of this week, share one insight from your tracker with a trusted colleague or direct report. Say something like: "I've been tracking my daily patterns, and I noticed that I tend to get most reactive on Mondays when I'm catching up from the weekend. If you see me getting intense on Monday mornings, would you mind checking in with me?"

This isn't about being vulnerable for the sake of it. It's about creating accountability and showing your team that self-awareness is valued and modeled from the top.

Tool 6: Inner Critic to Inner Coach Reframe

Remember that pattern you identified in Chapter 1's mirror work? This is where you start changing it. Use the same self-critical thought you discovered there as your starting point here.

Purpose: To challenge unhelpful thoughts and replace them with leadership-centered ones.

Instructions:

1. Write down a recurring thought from your inner critic. Example: "I'm terrible at leading this team."

2. Identify the impact of that thought. (How does it make you feel? Act?)

3. Reframe it as your inner coach would. Example: "I'm still learning, and I'm committed to getting better."

4. Practice the reframe daily. Say it out loud if you need to.

5. Write it down and hang it somewhere you can see it! Your brain is a creature of habit. Train it well.

Mirror Move: Reframing is a skill, but believing it? That takes evidence.

This week, choose one reframe you've written and act like it's true.

If your reframe says, "I'm still learning, and I'm committed to getting better," then prove it:

- Ask for feedback.

- Sign up for a learning opportunity - a course that builds on your strengths, a coaching program that will target your specific needs or join a mastermind with like-minded leaders.

- Take the lead on something that stretches you.

Track what happens, not just in the outcome, but in your mindset.

Because every time you lead from your inner coach instead of your inner critic, you're not just changing your thoughts. You're changing your story.

Tool 7: 5-Minute Mindset Reset

Purpose: To create a fast and effective pause during high-stress leadership moments.

Instructions: Set a timer for 5 minutes. Close the door. Put your phone down. Shut your computer cover. Then:

1. Breathe in for 4, hold for 4, exhale for 6. Repeat.

2. Ask: What story am I telling myself right now?

3. Ask: What do I need at this moment?

4. Ask: What's the next best step I can take as the leader I want to be?

That's it. Five minutes. Done consistently, this changes everything.

Mirror Move: One reset is good. A pattern of resets? That's leadership transformation.

This week, commit to doing the 5-Minute Mindset Reset once per day, especially when you feel stress rising. Track it using a simple log with these columns:

| Date | Situation | Story I Was Telling | My Reset Insight | Action Taken |

At the end of the week, review your log and reflect:

- Which triggers are repeat offenders?

- What reset insight came up the most?

- How did your actions shift once you paused?

If you can track it, you can change it. And when you consistently lead from a reset mind, people feel it, and results follow.

Final Thoughts: Leading yourself first

You have looked in the mirror and begun managing what you found there.

This is the completion of Pillar One, Clarity of Self.

You now understand something most leaders miss: what happens inside you always shows up outside you. Your thoughts shape your emotions. Your emotions shape your behavior. Your behavior shapes your results.

But awareness without structure will not sustain change.

That is where we go next.

Before you move on, pause for one final reflection:

What story is running your leadership right now, and is it serving you?

Pillar Two will help you protect and direct your energy so the leader you are becoming has the capacity to thrive.

CHAPTER THREE

Reset to Reclaim—Mastering Time and Energy

You don't need more hours. You need more intention.

This chapter takes you fully into the second pillar of The Leadership Mirror Framework, Mastering Time & Energy, where you learn to protect your capacity, your focus, and your ability to lead with intention.

Now we need to talk about the container that holds it all: your time and more importantly your energy.

All the self-awareness in the world won't matter if you're running on empty. You can't lead from clarity when you're operating from chaos. You can't be emotionally intelligent when you're emotionally depleted. And you certainly can't create the kind of intentional leadership we talked about in the first two chapters when you're stuck in survival mode.

Most leaders I work with aren't overwhelmed because they're doing the wrong things. They're overwhelmed because they're doing too many things at once, without pause, and without asking the one question that matters: Does this even matter?

The Fundamental Shift: From Time to Energy

We've been sold a lie. If you're not running on fumes, you're not working hard enough. If your calendar isn't packed, you're not important. If your inbox isn't overflowing, clearly, you're slacking.

That's not leadership. That's burnout with a badge.

Being busy isn't proof of value. It's a warning sign.

Every leader has a finite amount of mental, emotional, and physical energy. When you exceed that capacity consistently, you don't just get tired. You become reactive instead of responsive, snapping at people and making impulsive decisions. You become scattered instead of strategic, unable to hold the big picture because your brain is maxed out. You become defensive instead of curious, taking feedback as attacks because you lack the bandwidth to process it thoughtfully. You become controlling instead of empowering, micromanaging because you don't trust your depleted brain to delegate effectively.

This isn't a character flaw. This is what happens to human beings when they operate beyond their sustainable capacity.

The most powerful realization you can have as a leader: capacity is your most strategic resource.

You don't earn rest. You require it. You are not a machine. You're a human being leading other human beings.

Understanding Your Energy Reality

Before we can fix your energy management, we need to understand where your energy goes. Not your time. Your energy. There's a difference.

You might spend an hour in a meeting. If you spend three hours afterward replaying what you should have said differently then that meeting cost you four hours of energy.

Remember those mental energy drains from Chapter 2? Your inner critic, the replay loops, the catastrophizing? They all have external twins that amplify their impact:

- Decision Fatigue shows up when you're making every decision, big and small, while your team waits for direction.

- Context Switching happens when you jump from crisis to crisis without space to breathe or think.

- Emotional Labor accumulates when you carry everyone's stress, playing therapist and punching bag.

- Boundary Creep occurs when you say yes when your gut screams no, responding to emails at 9 PM.

- Perfectionism strikes when you rewrite the same email five times, obsessing over details that don't matter.

- Unfinished Business lingers in that conversation you keep avoiding, the decision you've been postponing.

- Technology Overwhelm builds with the constant ping of notifications, the compulsion to check "just once more."

These aren't just annoyances. They're leadership killers, draining your capacity one drop at a time.

When the Body Keeps Score

Sometimes we need to see the extreme to understand the everyday.

He was running the Latin American division of a global pharmaceutical company. Eighteen months into his dream role, he collapsed during a board presentation. Four hours of sleep, constant travel, conference room coffee as fuel. His body had been screaming warnings for months. He ignored them all.

The hospital tests revealed what he already knew yet wouldn't admit: adrenal exhaustion, dangerous blood pressure, pre-diabetic markers. The doctor didn't mince words: "Your body is done negotiating. You stop, or it stops you permanently."

Alejandro's recovery took a few months. Week One was nothing except sleep, fifteen hours a day. Week Two meant relearning to exist without producing, just walking and sitting in sunlight. By Week Three, he was writing about his daughters' laughs, things he hadn't noticed in years. Month Two became the great rejection, saying no to everything that didn't align with his values. By Month Three, he'd completely redesigned his approach. Energy replaced time as his primary metric.

"The irony," Alejandro told me, "is that I'm more successful now working fifty hours than I was working eighty. I had every warning sign. I ignored them because I thought that's what leadership demanded."

His final insight haunts me: "We tell ourselves we're irreplaceable. When I collapsed, the company didn't collapse. The machine kept running. The only thing that almost stopped permanently was me."

The Four Energy Zones

Alejandro's collapse was extreme, yet his pattern wasn't. Every leader moves through different combinations of energy and impact daily. Understanding where your activities fall helps you optimize your leadership effectiveness.

Building on the well-established energy/impact matrix, the principle is simple: maximize high-impact work, minimize low-impact work, regardless of energy required.

Think of it this way:

- Green Zone (High Energy, High Impact) is your peak performance zone where you're energized AND creating significant value. Strategic planning, critical decisions, breakthrough conversations with your team. This is where transformation happens.

- Yellow Zone (Low Energy, High Impact) is your efficiency zone. The work still matters, but you've built systems that make it flow. Running structured meetings, reviewing properly delegated work, using templates you've created. Good processes make this zone powerful.

- Red Zone (High Energy, Low Impact) is the danger zone. You're working hard but creating little value. Redoing work that wasn't delegated properly, attending meetings where you add no unique value, perfectionist editing of low-priority communications. This is where energy bleeds out.

- Gray Zone (Low Energy, Low Impact) is organizational waste. Sitting through irrelevant presentations, maintaining outdated processes nobody questions, administrative tasks that could be automated or eliminated. Pure drain, no gain.

Most leaders are surprised when they track their actual time allocation. They discover they're spending far less time than they thought in Green Zone, with too much energy scattered across Red Zone activities that feel urgent but create little value. The shift to more Green Zone time happens through deliberate choices, better delegation, and the courage to say no to low-impact work, regardless of how much energy it demands.

The goal isn't perfection. It's awareness followed by intentional shifts. When you know which zone you're in, you can make conscious choices about whether to stay there or move.

(See Tool 8: Energy Zone Optimization at the end of this chapter for a detailed assessment and strategies to maximize your time in high-impact zones.)

Designing Your Energy System

Understanding your zones is step one. Step two is designing your life to honor them.

Start with your calendar. Open it right now. Does it reflect someone who knows their values and priorities? Or does it reveal a leader drowning in other people's agendas, attending meetings that don't matter, solving problems others should own?

When you don't protect your time and energy, someone else will do it for you. And you probably won't like their plan.

I learned this lesson the hard way. For years, I prided myself on being available to everyone, sleeping three hours during big projects, wearing exhaustion like a medal. My coach introduced me to something that changed everything: reset rituals.

Not spa days or meditation retreats. Simple, repeatable practices that take minutes yet save hours. Ten minutes at day's end noting what energized versus drained me. One-minute breathing pauses between meetings. A weekly check-in with myself before my priorities got hijacked.

These tiny rituals transformed how I led. I stopped letting my days happen to me and started designing them deliberately.

The same principle applies to delegation. Every minute you spend doing work someone else could handle is a minute stolen from work only you can do. Training someone takes time, yes. They might do it differently, yes. If you don't delegate, though, you'll never escape the Yellow Zone. You'll be that leader who's always busy, never strategic. Always working, never growing.

The question isn't whether you have time to delegate. It's whether you have time not to.

The Meeting Problem (And How to Sell the Solution)

Of all the energy drains leaders face, one stands above the rest: meetings.

The average executive spends 23 hours weekly in meetings. I worked with a leadership team spending 70% of their time in meetings, repeatedly discussing the same issues over and over again without any resolution or decision. Sound familiar?

You probably aren't the one calling all these meetings. Your boss is. Or their boss is. Or one of your peers. Before you can fix this, you need to get buy-in from above. If you feel this pain and want to do something about it, I suggest completing the Meeting Transformation Audit (Tool 9 below).

Then comes the hard part, you must take it to the leadership above you. Here are some strategies that have worked with my clients.

First, lead with data, not complaints. Don't say "We have too many meetings." Say "I analyzed our team's time allocation. We're spending 16 hours weekly in unnecessary meetings, which costs approximately $1,312,000 annually in salary time. I have a proposal to reclaim 6 of those hours for strategic work while improving our decision quality." Your boss responds to business metrics, not frustration.

Second, present a pilot, not a revolution. Don't propose dismantling the entire meeting structure. Your boss will panic about losing control. Instead, suggest: "Could we pilot a new approach for 30 days with just the Tuesday operations meeting? If it works, we can expand. If not, we revert." Low risk, high potential reward. That's a yes.

Third, frame it as optimization, not elimination. Your boss likely believes meetings equal alignment. Show how better meetings create better alignment. One Decision, One Meeting prevents decision recycling and speeds execution. Pre-read requirements elevate discussion quality. A 45-minute default improves focus and energy. You're not anti-meeting. You're pro-effectiveness.

Finally, connect to what they care about. Listen to what keeps your boss up at night, then connect meeting reform to that. "This would free 6 hours weekly for the digital transformation you've been pushing." Or "Faster decisions would help us beat competitor X to market." Make it their win, not yours.

When they push back (and they will), be ready. If they say it's too risky, respond: "That's exactly why I'm suggesting a 30-day pilot with one meeting. We can measure impact before making permanent changes." If they insist on alignment, agree: "Better meetings create better alignment. When decisions stick the first time, we move faster together."

The secret is positioning this as making your boss look like an innovative leader who gets more from their team without burning them out. When they look good to their boss because the team is executing faster, you'll get all the support you need.

Managing Energy Vampires

We all know them. Some people consistently drain your energy while others restore it.

Energy vampires complain without seeking solutions, create drama where none exists, demand constant reassurance, push their anxiety onto you, never take ownership.

Energy generators bring solutions alongside problems, take ownership of outcomes, communicate directly, support team success, challenge you to grow.

You can't eliminate every energy vampire from your work life. You can minimize their impact by setting clear boundaries ("I have ten minutes, then I need to focus on the client meeting"), limiting access (create office hours for drop-ins), addressing patterns directly ("This behavior is affecting the team. What's behind it?") and spending more time with people who multiply your energy rather than drain it.

Your energy is finite yet renewable. Protect it accordingly.

The Compound Effect

Consistent energy management creates predictable results:

- Week 1: You feel less overwhelmed

- Month 1: Your team notices you're more present

- Month 3: Strategic thinking returns

- Month 6: Your leadership becomes the model others follow

This isn't about perfect time management. It's about intentional energy stewardship. Small changes compound into transformation.

Your Turn: Tools to Reclaim Your Energy

The tools in this chapter will ask more from you than any others in the book. They take time, attention, and honesty. They may feel tedious at first, because they require you to slow down, observe your patterns, and look closely at where your energy is actually going. But they will also give you some of the most powerful returns you will experience as a leader.

If you commit to these tools, even for a short period of time, you will uncover what has been draining you, what has been distracting you, and what has been holding you back from doing your highest value work. Most leaders finish this process surprised, relieved, and sometimes a little embarrassed by what they discover. That is normal. The audit tells the truth, and the truth is what gives you power.

There are two tools in this chapter, and each has a companion worksheet available as a free download at www.theleadershipmirror. com. Do not rush them. The value comes from paying attention long enough to see the patterns clearly. Give yourself the same focus you give your team. You are worth that investment.

If you are willing to do the work, these tools will help you reclaim your time, rebuild your energy, and create space for the leadership you want to practice. Let's begin.

Tool 8: Energy Zone Optimization

Daily Tracking Log:

Time	Activity	Energy Required (H/L)	Impact Created (H/L)	Zone	Notes
8:00–9:00	Email processing	L	L	Gray	Could batch this
9:00–10:30	Strategic planning session	H	H	Green	Felt energized
10:30–11:00	Status meeting	H	L	Red	Why was I there?
11:00–12:00	1-on-1 with direct report	L	H	Yellow	Good systems in place

Purpose: To understand where your time actually goes and make one intentional shift toward higher-impact leadership.

This tool has depth. Do not try to do everything at once.

Start with awareness.

Step 1: Three-Day Energy Audit

For the next three days, track every activity that takes 15 minutes or more.

Do not change your behavior. Just observe.

Use this framework:

- Green = High Energy + High Impact
  Your best leadership work. Strategic thinking.
  Meaningful conversations. Real progress.

- Yellow = Low Energy + High Impact
  Important work that supports results but does
  not energize you. Reviews. Structured meetings.
  Planning. Necessary administration.

- Red = High Energy + Low Impact
  Urgent, reactive, busy work. Feels productive but
  moves little.

- Gray = Low Energy + Low Impact
  Draining and unnecessary. The work you question
  later.

Yellow is not the enemy. It is the discipline zone. When managed well, it supports Green. When unmanaged, it quietly drains you.

After three days, total your hours in each zone.

Most leaders discover they spend far less time in Green than they assumed.

Example Daily Tracking Log

Time	Activity	Energy Required (H/L)	Impact Created (H/L)	Zone	Notes
8:00–9:00	Email processing	L	L	Gray	Could batch this
9:00–10:30	Strategic planning session	H	H	Green	Felt energized
10:30–11:00	Status meeting	H	L	Red	Why was I there?
11:00–12:00	1-on-1 with direct report	L	H	Yellow	Good systems in place

Step 2: Notice the Pattern

You are not redesigning your life. You are identifying leverage.

Ask:

- When do I naturally land in Green?

- What consistently pushes me into Red?

- What Gray tasks keep reappearing?

- Where is Yellow necessary but inefficient?

Awareness first. Optimization second.

Step 3: Make One Shift

Choose one of the following:

- Move one recurring Red task into Yellow by adding structure.

- Eliminate or delegate one Gray activity.

- Protect one additional Green block next week.

That is enough to begin.

Small shifts compound.

Step 4: Protect Green Intentionally

Over time, aim for this direction (not perfection):

- Green: Majority of your focused leadership time

- Yellow: Structured and contained

- Red: Limited and intentional

- Gray: Minimal

If Green is not scheduled, it will disappear. If you do not design your week, others will design it for you.

Step 5: Sustain the Practice

Each week, ask:

- What percentage of my time was Green?

- What pushed me into Red?

- What enabled Green?

- What one adjustment would improve next week?

Progress matters more than precision.

Mirror Move:

After completing your audit, share one insight with someone you trust.

Ask them:

- "Where do you see me adding the most value?"

- "Where do you see me wasting energy?"

Then implement one change within the next seven days.

Awareness without action fades.

Action If you are willing to do the work, these tools will help you reclaim your time, rebuild your energy, and create space for the leadership you want to practice. Let's begin.

Commitment

I will track my energy for three days starting: ___________

My one priority shift will be: __________

I will protect ______ hours of Green time next week.

Now stop reading and start tracking.

The mirror of your calendar is waiting.

Tool 9: Meeting Transformation Audit

Meeting Tracking Log:

Mon	Weekly Status	60 min	12	Listener	No	No	Yes	Drained
Mon	Budget Review	90 min	6	Contributor	Yes	Yes	No	Neutral
Tue	"Quick" sync	45 min	3	Required?	No	No	Yes	Frustrated

Purpose: To uncover how much time your meetings actually consume and make one data-driven improvement.

You do not need to fix every meeting. Start with awareness. Then change one.

Step 1: One-Week Reality Check

For one week, track every meeting longer than 10 minutes. After each meeting, rate it:

- Energized

- Neutral

- Drained

- Angry

At the end of the week, calculate:

- Total hours in meetings

- Hours that resulted in clear decisions

- Hours that could have been handled asynchronously

- Hours where you added unique value

Most leaders are surprised by the gap between time spent and value created.

Example Meeting Tracking Log

Day	Meeting Name	Duration	Attendees	Your Role?	Clear?	Mode?	Email?	Impact
Mon	Weekly Status	60 min	12	Listener	No	No	Yes	Drained
Mon	Budget Review	90 min	6	Contributor	Yes	Yes	No	Neutral
Tue	"Quick" sync	45 min	3	Required?	No	No	Yes	Frustrated

Step 2: Identify the Pattern

Ask:

- Which meetings consistently drain energy?
- Which exist for information sharing only?
- Which require real-time discussion?
- Where am I present but not necessary?

You are not eliminating everything. You are identifying waste.

Step 3: Choose One Meeting to Transform

Do not overhaul your calendar.

Pick one recurring meeting.

For that meeting, make one or more of these changes:

- Shorten it.
- Reduce the attendee list.
- Add a clear purpose statement.
- Require pre-reads.
- End with documented decisions and owners.

- Clarity improves meetings more than duration.

Step 4: Make the Cost Visible (Optional but Powerful)

If you want leverage, calculate this:

- Meeting duration × number of attendees × average hourly rate.
- That number changes the conversation.
- Leaders respond to data.

Step 5: Run a 30-Day Pilot

Test your changes for 30 days.
Track:

- Time saved
- Decisions made
- Team energy feedback

If alignment drops, adjust. If clarity improves, expand.

Mirror Move: Choose the worst-rated meeting from your audit.

At the start of the next session, say:

"I'm working to make this meeting more valuable. What is one change that would improve it?"

Then implement one suggestion immediately.

Leadership credibility grows when people see you respond.

Final Thoughts: The Choice Point

You just learned something many leaders never fully grasp. Time management is not the solution. Energy management is.

You may have started this chapter trying to control your calendar. Now you understand the real issue was not time. It was where your energy was going and how much of it was leaking into work that does not matter.

Insight alone will not change that.

Many leaders will read this, nod, and return to the same Red Zone meetings and the same hijacked priorities. Nothing shifts unless you decide it will.

So decide.

Not next month. Not when things slow down. Now.

Choose one action from this chapter and take it before you move on:

- Cancel one meeting that adds no value.

- Protect one two-hour Green Zone block this week.

- Redesign one recurring Red Zone drain.

- Create a five-minute daily reset to review what energized and depleted you.

The first time you protect your energy, it may feel uncomfortable. You may feel guilty. Do it anyway.

Nothing will collapse.

But something will change.

When you reclaim even thirty minutes and protect it, you prove to yourself that you are capable of directing your energy instead of reacting to everyone else's demands.

That is the shift.

Energy management is not selfish. It is strategic.

Your team benefits from a leader who is clear instead of depleted. Your organization benefits from focused work instead of constant urgency.

Open your calendar.

Find one Red or Gray commitment this week. Shorten it. Delegate it. Eliminate it. Protect the time.

Then make it specific:

This week at [time], I will [action] to protect energy for [higher-impact work].

Write it down.

Do it before you turn the page.

Because knowing what would improve your leadership and refusing to act on it is a choice.

Are you ready to choose differently?

Pillar Three, Culture by Design, builds on this capacity. The energy you reclaim now becomes the foundation for the environment you create next.

CHAPTER FOUR

Culture by Design

You might be thinking, "The culture of our organization is tough. I can't change it."

Let me share what happened with a client who said exactly that. We spent two weeks identifying what was actually within their control, and they were surprised by how much they could influence.

By culture, I mean the shared beliefs, behaviors, and expectations that shape how work gets done and how people treat one another. It shows up in decisions, pace, tone, norms, and what gets rewarded or tolerated.

While you might not change your entire organizational culture, you absolutely can shift the culture within your span of control. When you do, something interesting happens: others notice the changes and start asking what you did differently.

What you can change within your span of control:

- Meeting norms on your team

- How decisions are made and documented

- Clarity of roles, expectations, and standards

- How conflict is handled

- How feedback is given and received

- Recognition and how wins are celebrated

- Boundaries that protect focus and well-being

- Who is in the room for key conversations

What you likely cannot change alone:

- Company-wide compensation structures

- Enterprise policies and legal constraints

- Executive strategies you do not own

- Legacy systems and budgets you do not control

- Organization-wide performance processes and tools

Bottom line: You can change the climate people experience when they work with you. That's where culture by design starts. And often, that's where organizational change begins too, with one leader deciding to do things differently.

This chapter focuses on the third pillar of The Leadership Mirror Framework, Culture by Design. Here you will learn how to shape the environment within your span of control so that people experience your values, not just hear you talk about them.

Know this: You already shape the culture. Good or bad, you shape it. The real opportunity is to shape it on purpose with clarity, courage, and alignment to what matters most.

Culture isn't a slogan on the wall or a slide in the onboarding deck. Culture is how people feel when they walk into a room with you.

It's how decisions get made, how conflict gets handled, how wins get celebrated (or ignored). It's how safe, or unsafe, it feels to speak up, take risks, or just be human.

And here's the part most leaders overlook you are always influencing culture, even when you're not trying to. Especially when you're not trying to.

So, the real question isn't whether you're shaping culture. It's *how* you're shaping it.

Are you doing it by design? Or by default?

From Energy to Environment

In Chapter 3, you learned to protect and manage your energy. You discovered which zones drain you and which ones energize you. Now we're going to explore what happens with that reclaimed energy.

When you're not exhausted, you notice things. When you're not in survival mode, you can be intentional. When you're operating from your Green Zone, you have the capacity to shape the environment around you.

Think about it. Every interaction you have either builds or erodes culture. But when you're depleted (Red Zone), those interactions tend to be reactive, terse, or checked out. When you're energized and present, those same interactions become opportunities to reinforce what matters.

Your energy state directly impacts your culture-shaping ability. That's why the inner work comes first. Now that you've reclaimed your capacity, let's talk about how to use it.

The Accidental Culture Trap

I've worked with too many leaders who say, "We need to fix the culture around here," as if culture is some fog hovering above the team.

But culture isn't "out there." It's right here. It's in every meeting, every choice, every moment. And it starts with you.

You model the behavior. You reward or tolerate what happens. You create clarity or confusion. You build trust or you break it.

One project in particular drove this home for me.

Thanksgiving in Botswana: Choosing Culture on Purpose

In Botswana, the team was exhausted. Morale had dropped. The work was still moving, but people were frayed. Some were talking about going home early. The holidays were approaching, which only made the weight of the experience heavier.

I could have focused on deadlines. I could have pushed harder for results. That was the version of leadership I once believed in. Results first. People second. But I knew that pushing would only break what was already fragile. What we needed was not more pressure. We needed connection.

So, we decided to do something bold. We decided to bring Thanksgiving to Botswana.

When I told the hotel manager what we wanted to do, she looked at me with a mixture of confusion and disbelief. "You want to cook American Thanksgiving dinner? Here? With ingredients we do not have?"

"Yes," I said. "That is exactly what we want to do."

What followed was a logistical adventure that became somewhat of a turning point for all of us. The hotel staff jumped in without hesitation. Someone knew someone who could get a turkey. Another person had access to cranberries. Spices were tracked down. We improvised stuffing (or dressing depending on where you are from). Sean's Mac & Cheese were one of the favorites! Everyone contributed something.

Our team submitted favorite family recipes, and the chefs did their best to recreate each one. The hotel staff became part of our team for the week. There was laughter again. Collaboration again. A sense of anticipation that we had not felt in months.

This was before cell phone cameras were everywhere, so we do not have pictures. But the memory is vivid. We sat for hours.

There was no pressure and no talk about deadlines. Just food, stories, and genuine connection. It was exactly what Thanksgiving was meant to be.

That night something changed. It did not fix everything, but it restored something essential. People felt seen and valued again. They felt grounded and connected to one another, not just to the work. Leadership did not feel like a burden that day. It felt like a privilege. I still get messages from team members on Thanksgiving reminding me of that night.

That dinner taught me something I have carried into every leadership engagement since. Culture is not created by accident. It is shaped by leaders who choose humanity when the moment calls for it. It reminded me that you do not create a healthy culture by talking about values. You create it by creating experiences that show people they matter.

The Truth About Leadership and Culture

That experience in Botswana showed me what becomes possible when leaders create culture on purpose. It was not a strategic plan or a formal initiative. It was a simple, human decision to bring people together in a moment when everything felt overwhelming. It reminded me that culture is shaped long before the big milestones. It is shaped in the everyday choices leaders make when no one is watching.

But I have also seen the opposite. I have seen what happens when leaders ignore the impact they have on the emotional climate of their team. Some blame the culture as if it is an external force. Others assume that if they talk about values often enough, the team will absorb them through osmosis. But culture does not reflect what a leader says. It reflects how a leader behaves.

If your team is afraid, disengaged, or burned out, you cannot point to culture as the culprit. Culture is not something outside of you. It is a mirror of you. It reveals whether people feel safe or silenced. It shows whether your team feels trusted or micromanaged. It reflects your tone, your presence, and your consistency.

Many leaders resist this idea because it feels like too much responsibility. But the truth is freeing. You shape the culture, which means you can change it. You can influence what people experience simply by choosing to show up differently.

Before blaming the team or the pressure or the environment, ask yourself the hard questions:

- How am I showing up right now?

- What behaviors am I modeling, intentionally or not?

- How is my mood shaping the room?

- What tone am I setting without realizing it?

- What fears, expectations, or habits might I be passing on to my team?

Instead of assuming others do not "get it," pause long enough to get curious. Ask for genuine feedback and listen with the intention to understand, not defend. You cannot claim to value honesty while creating an environment where people feel punished for telling you the truth.

When leaders are willing to shift their mindset, everything can change. Here is what that shift often looks like:

- Setting a clear vision and inviting the team into it.

- Creating space for pushback and making it clear that honesty is expected.

- Acknowledging the pressure you feel without making it an excuse for poor behavior.

- Modeling calm when stress rises so the team does not absorb your anxiety.
- Treating consultants, peers, or direct reports as partners instead of threats.

The culture will follow. Because culture is not built by memos or mandates. It is built by the behavior people see every day.

You do not need to have all the answers. What matters is leading in a way that honors both people and performance. Curiosity over control. Listening before directing. Partnership instead of fear.

Culture is built in micro-moments. Simple (maybe not easy) things that many leaders overlook:

- Open meetings with a clear purpose and the decision you aim to make.
- Name the real issue instead of circling around it.
- Stop interruptions and make space for quieter voices.
- Close the loop on decisions so people know what comes next.
- Celebrate learning, not only outcomes, especially when someone takes a risk.
- Give credit in public and give tough feedback in private.
- Ask one powerful question before giving one directive.
- Protect focused work time and explain why it matters.
- Respond to mistakes with inquiry first, then action.
- Document team norms and revisit them when they drift.

These small choices compound. They form the emotional climate of a team. They teach people what to expect from you and from one another. They determine whether people bring their best ideas or keep their heads down. That is the real power of culture. It pulls people toward their potential or pushes them into survival mode.

You do not need a three-day retreat to change culture. You do not need a slogan or a handbook. You need awareness. You need courage. You need to decide that how you lead matters, because it does.

Culture is not an accident waiting to happen. It is a choice. One you make every day, in every conversation, in every room you enter.

What You Permit, You Promote

One of the most important lessons I've ever learned came from watching what happens when leaders stay silent.
You know the moments:

- A team member rolls their eyes in a meeting.

- Someone interrupts repeatedly.

- A high performer bullies their way to results.

And the leader says nothing.

That silence? That's not neutral. It's permission. And over time, permission becomes culture.

As a leader, silence is a signal. If you don't speak up, you're saying this is fine. This is acceptable. This is who we are.

One of my clients, Mike, was a manager at a large manufacturing company. He worked his way up for more than twenty years. People respected him because he was steady, knew the work, and let people do their jobs without breathing down their necks.

But over time, he started to notice things shifting. Meetings felt tense. Communication between shifts was breaking down. And some of the most reliable team members were pulling back. One of his top employees left without much explanation.

In one of our coaching conversations, he mentioned a technician named Harold. Harold was good and knew the systems better than anyone, but he had a way of shutting others down. Harold acted like he was the smartest guy in the room. He talked over people and made sarcastic comments when someone asked a question. No one addressed it, including Mike.

I asked him, "Have you talked to Harold about how he shows up?"

Mike paused. "Not directly. I figured everyone knew that's just how he is. He's old school."

Then I asked, "What do you think your silence is saying?"

He sat with that for a moment. "It probably tells the team it's okay."

Things shifted. Mike had a direct conversation with Harold. He told him that his behavior was affecting the team and that it had to change. He reminded Harold that he was a trusted member of the team and that his behavior was impacting other team members. After some back and forth Harold understood the impact of his behavior and vowed to do better.

Mike then clarified expectations during a team huddle. He told the team he had let some things slide that didn't reflect the kind of environment they were trying to build, and that it was on him to fix it.

That simple moment of clarity reset the tone. People started speaking up again. The team felt more focused. Harold, once he understood the behavior and his impact on the team, made an effort to be more respectful.

Later, Mike told me, "I thought saying nothing kept things smooth. But really, I was letting the wrong things take root."

Do you notice inappropriate or misaligned behaviors on your team?

Culture by design requires clarity:

- What do you stand for?

- What will you not tolerate?

- Are those values just words or are they visible in the way you lead?

Modeling the Way (Even When It's Hard)

You cannot call for accountability and never own your own mistakes. You cannot preach transparency and then keep people in the dark. You cannot ask for trust while holding all the control.

One of the fastest ways to shift culture is to model what you expect.

- Want culture of feedback? Ask for it and respond with curiosity.

- Want innovation? Celebrate risk, not just results.

- Want well-being? Take a break. A real one. And don't apologize for it.

People don't need a mission statement. They need a model. And that model is you.

Your team will do as you do. They will act as you act. Whether you realize it or not, they're watching and mirroring.

I know some of you might push back on that. But think of it this way: maybe it's not the sharp, high-def mirror hanging in your bathroom. Maybe it's more like your grandma's old mirror, warped around the edges, but still showing you the truth.

If you're stressed, your team feels it. If you're working long hours, so are they. If you use meetings to spread blame, dodge accountability, or rope others into your drama, don't be surprised when they follow suit.

The good news? The mirror works both ways.

When you start showing up with ownership, authenticity, and care, your team reflects that too. I was getting results but people were shrinking around me. Once I realized the ripple effect I was creating, I changed how I showed up. I engaged more intentionally with the teams I worked with. I stopped going through the motions and started listening. I showed them I cared not just about the work, but about them as people. Their contributions. Their challenges. Their wins.

And it changed everything.

They felt seen. Valued. Heard. Their performance improved. Their energy shifted. We moved faster and we moved together.

You can do the same. I'm not saying you can flip a switch and go from feared to trusted overnight. If you suddenly start showing up differently, your team might be skeptical. Or think you've gone crazy. They'll wonder if there's a hidden agenda. That's okay. Be honest with them. Tell them you're working on your leadership and one of the things you're focused on is building stronger relationships.

Start small. Build trust slowly. Begin with your informal leaders, the ones others look to before they look to you. They'll help carry the change forward, one step at a time.

Trust Builds the Culture for Feedback

You don't get to opt out of shaping culture. Every interaction shapes it, whether you realize it or not. The real question is: are you proud of the culture you're creating?

You cannot control everything that happens on your team, but you can control how you lead through it. When your leadership consistently reflects your values, people believe in more than just the work. They believe in the way you work together.

The Anatomy of Trust

Trust doesn't happen by accident. It's built through consistent actions over time. When your team trusts you, they'll tell you what's really happening, not what they think you want to hear.

Consider what trust actually requires:

- Reliability isn't just meeting deadlines. It's being the same leader whether things are going well or falling apart. Your team needs to know which version of you will show up. When you're consistent in your responses, even under pressure, people stop walking on eggshells and start bringing real issues forward.

- Honesty isn't just not lying. It's sharing what you can when you can, admitting what you don't know, and explaining the "why" behind decisions. When you can't share everything (and sometimes you can't), say that. "I can't share all the details yet, but here's what I can tell you..." builds more trust than silence or vague promises.

- Being "for them" isn't cheerleading. It's making tough decisions that serve their growth, even when it's uncomfortable. Sometimes being for someone means giving them feedback they don't want to hear. Sometimes it means protecting them from organizational chaos. Sometimes it means pushing them toward a challenge they don't think they're ready for.

Trust in Practice

Nate inherited a team that had been burned by their previous leader's broken promises. They'd been told promotions were coming (they weren't), that their project was priority (it got defunded), that their input mattered (it was ignored).

Nate knew he couldn't just declare "trust me" and expect it to work. Instead, he started small:

- He made modest commitments and kept them.

- When he couldn't deliver something, he explained why immediately.

- He shared his own struggles and uncertainties appropriately.

- He asked for their input and showed exactly how it influenced decisions.

After three months, one team member told him: "You're the first boss who does what they say they'll do. Even the small stuff."

That's how trust builds. Not through headline moments, but through accumulated evidence that you're worthy of it.

Building a Feedback Culture That Works

A culture of feedback isn't about performance forms or annual reviews. It's a workplace where people feel safe to speak up, share ideas, and challenge each other because they trust each other's intentions. Feedback becomes a daily rhythm, not an annual ritual. It's how learning happens in real time, not after the fact.

In a culture of feedback:

- People give feedback because they care, not because they're frustrated.

- Leaders ask for feedback first and model how to receive it well.

- Teams talk about what's working and what's not before it becomes a crisis.

Here's what it takes:

- Ask for feedback and thank people for it.

- Accept the feedback you don't like with grace, and don't punish people for giving it to you.

- Change what you can change as a result of what you hear.

- Normalize conflict. It isn't a problem; it's a path to clarity.

- Give feedback in real time, not once a year.

- Build safety first. Feedback without trust is just noise.

Where Trust and Truth Collide

Culture by design tells the truth. Even when it's uncomfortable. Even when it's messy. Especially then.

Trust makes that possible. Feedback makes it sustainable.

When feedback becomes part of how the team operates with each other, not just how they operate with you, you've built something sustainable.

Creating a feedback-rich culture isn't about being nice. It's about being clear. It's about being brave enough to name the real stuff, and humble enough to hear it.

What would happen if feedback was done not as an annual ritual, but as part of the daily rhythm of truth-telling that shapes your team?

If your team can't speak openly, push back on ideas, or surface hard truths, that isn't a healthy culture. That's control.

And that's how blind spots turn into barriers.

Your Turn: Tools to Build Culture Intentionally

Let's move from insight to action. These tools will help you take responsibility for the culture you're shaping, moment by moment.

Tool 10: Culture Touchpoints Inventory

Purpose: To identify where your leadership is reinforcing (or eroding) the culture you want.

Instructions: Review the following culture touchpoints and reflect:

- Team meetings
- One-on-ones
- Emails and communication tone
- Decision-making processes
- Recognition and feedback
- Onboarding and offboarding

Ask:

- What are these touchpoints communicating about our culture?

- Where is there a gap between what we *say* we value and what we *actually* do?
- What's one touchpoint I can redesign this week to better reflect my leadership values?

This tool helps you lead culture *by design*, not default.

Mirror Move: Pick your biggest culture gap from the inventory and bring it to your team openly. Don't sugarcoat it.

Try this script: "I've been looking at how we actually operate versus what we say we value, and I found a gap. In our touchpoint around [specific area], we're sending mixed messages. Here's what I'm seeing..."

Then ask: "What are you noticing? Where else might we be saying one thing but doing another?"

Make it a standing agenda item for the next month. Every team meeting spend 10 minutes on one touchpoint. Ask: "How did this go this week? What did it communicate about who we are?"

When leaders get honest about cultural gaps, teams stop pretending they don't exist too.

Tool 11: Model the Way Checklist

Purpose: To get honest about how well you're living the values you expect from others.

Instructions: Pick 3 values you want to define your team's culture. For each one, ask:

- How do I model this value daily?
- Where have I been inconsistent?
- What's one concrete behavior I can commit to this week to lead more clearly?

Example:

- Value: Trust
- I delegate decisions.
- I micromanage under pressure.
- Action: Let go of final approval on two low stakes tasks this week.

Consistency builds credibility.

Mirror Move: Modeling works best when people can see it happening.

Take your weekly behavior commitment and make it visible. Tell your team exactly what you're working on and why.

For example: "I realized I say I value trust, but I still want final approval on too many decisions. This week, I'm letting go of signing off on [specific tasks]. If you see me slipping back into old habits, call me on it."

Then follow through publicly. In your next team meeting, report back: "Here's how I did this week. Here's where I succeeded, here's where I didn't, and here's what I'm adjusting."

Ask your team: "What value do you want to model better? How can we support each other in living what we say matters?"

Vulnerability about your own growth gives others permission to grow too.

Tool 12: Feedback Loops that Build Trust

Purpose: To create real-time, two-way feedback rhythms on your team.

Instructions: Start simple:

- In your next team meeting, ask:
  "What's one thing I could do differently as your leader to better support you?"

- In your next 1:1, ask:
  "What's something I might not be seeing that I should pay attention to?"
- For yourself:
  "What feedback am I avoiding giving and why?"

Then act on it. Don't just say, "thank you", show you heard it.

The fastest way to build a culture of honesty is to be honest first.

Mirror Move: Real feedback culture happens when it flows in all directions, not just down from you.

After you've asked for feedback and acted on it, flip it. Train your team to give each other the same quality of feedback they're giving you.

In your next team meeting: "Last week you told me [specific feedback] and I [specific action taken]. Now I want us to practice this with each other."

Set up peer feedback pairs or small groups. Give them the same prompts: "What's one thing I could do differently to better support you?" and "What's something I might not be seeing?"

Final Thoughts: Culture Doesn't Happen By Accident

You now have another concept many leaders never grasp - culture isn't something that happens to you. It's something you create with every interaction, every decision, every moment of leadership.

Think about where this chapter started. You might have believed culture was set in stone, determined by executives or traditions you couldn't influence. Now you understand that within your span of control, you ARE the culture.

When you permit behavior through silence, you promote it. When you model what you expect, you multiply it. When you build trust through consistency, you enable the kind of honest feedback that makes teams exceptional.

The tools in this chapter aren't just exercises. They're practices that, when used consistently, transform how people experience work. Your Culture Touchpoints Inventory reveals where reality doesn't match rhetoric. Your Model the Way Checklist ensures you're leading by example. Your Feedback Loops create the psychological safety that enables growth.

Perhaps most importantly, you now understand that culture change doesn't require permission from above or a company-wide initiative. It starts with you deciding that within your sphere of influence, things will be different.

Chapter 5 will show you how this intentional culture work naturally expands your influence. When people experience a different way of working with you, one built on trust, clarity, and genuine care, word spreads. Your influence grows not through politics or positioning, but through the simple power of creating an environment where people thrive.

For now, pick one culture element you want to shift. Maybe it's how meetings start. Maybe it's how feedback flows. Maybe it's how mistakes are handled. Choose one thing and change it this week.

Because culture by design isn't a someday project. It's a today decision that shapes every tomorrow.

Ready to expand your influence?

The culture is yours to shape.

CHAPTER FIVE

Grow Your Influence, Expand Your Impact

The most effective leaders don't control outcomes; they create ripples that extend far beyond what they can see. When you influence through trust and connection, your impact multiplies exponentially.

By the time you reach this point, you have invested real effort in understanding your leadership.

You've looked inward. You've challenged old habits. You've reclaimed your time, your energy, and your sense of self. You've learned to design culture instead of letting it happen by default.

Now it's time to lead outward. To grow your influence and expand your impact.

With this chapter, you are stepping into the fourth pillar of The Leadership Mirror Framework, Expanding Influence and Impact. Over the next chapters, you will learn how to lead beyond yourself and create ripples of positive change that last.

This chapter isn't about visibility or climbing the ladder faster. It's about leading in a way that is felt, remembered, and multiplied. Influence is how leaders extend their reach. Impact is how they change the game.

This is how it looks in practice.

Influence That Ripples

You may have worked for a leader like Laura, a mid-level director of a manufacturing company known for its cutthroat culture. When Laura took over her team, she inherited what everyone called "the problem department". There was high turnover, missed deadlines, and a reputation for drama.

The company culture rewarded individual achievement over collaboration. People hoarded information, threw each other under the bus in meetings, and measured success by who could work the longest hours. Laura had climbed the ladder by playing this game, but watching her team burn out made her question everything.

Instead of continuing the cycle, Laura decided to design her team's culture intentionally. She started small.

She began every team meeting by asking, "What's going well that we should celebrate?" She implemented "failure parties" where the team analyzed mistakes without blame. She started protecting her people from unnecessary meetings and unrealistic deadlines. She made it safe to say, "I don't know" or "I need help."

At first, other departments mocked her approach. "Laura's team has gone soft," they said. But something interesting started happening.

Laura's team began hitting their targets consistently. Their quality metrics improved. People stopped calling in sick or looking for transfers. They started innovating and taking initiative in ways that surprised everyone.

Six months later, other department heads began asking Laura what she was doing differently. Her boss started referencing her team as the model for others. HR asked her to share her approach at the leadership retreat. People from other companies who heard about her team's transformation started reaching out for advice.

Laura hadn't been trying to build influence. She'd been focused on building her team. But influence found her anyway.

That's how real influence works. It's not something you chase. It's something you earn through how you lead every single day.

Let's get clear on what influence is and what it isn't.

What is Influence?

Influence is not about volume, title, or personality. It is not about dominating meetings or charming people into agreement. Real influence is earned through how you show up day after day. It is built in the small moments: how you follow through, how you handle pressure, and how you treat those who have nothing to offer you.

People do not need a perfect leader. They need a trustworthy one. They will follow a leader who makes mistakes. They will not follow one who breaks trust and refuses to own it.

Influence becomes visible when people lean in as you speak, pause when you challenge an idea, or shift their energy simply because they respect the way you lead. It grows from credibility, consistency, and connection, not from authority or position. Influence does not require permission. It requires trust.

The Difference Between Influence and Authority

To see the difference clearly, look at two leaders with the same title.

Tom had all the symbols of authority. Corner office. Executive assistant. Direct access to senior leadership. When he wanted something done, he sent emails marked urgent and escalated quickly when people moved slowly. He got compliance, but never commitment. The moment he left the room, people rolled their eyes.

Michelle led very differently. She explained why things mattered. She asked for input. She took responsibility when things went wrong and shared credit when things went right. Her team did not work late because they had to. They did it because they wanted to.

Authority gets short-term obedience. Influence creates long-term loyalty. Authority ends where your title ends. Influence travels with you wherever you go.

Tom led from authority. Michelle led from influence.

Authority stops where your title ends. Influence travels with you wherever you go.

The Influence Trifecta: Credibility. Consistency. Connection.

Lasting influence rests on three foundations:

- Credibility comes from competence and integrity, from being someone whose judgment can be trusted.

- Consistency creates psychological safety, so people know who they'll get no matter the pressure.

- Connection humanizes leadership, reminding people they matter, not just what they deliver.

Think of these as the legs of a stool. Remove one, and your influence wobbles.

I learned this the hard way on a project that was falling apart. My instinct was to push harder and fix faster, but none of that worked. So I tried something different. I told the truth.

"I am struggling here," I said. "This project is not going the way any of us hoped. I need your help figuring out how to get it back on track."

The room was quiet at first. Then people started telling the truth. They named the broken processes and the resource gaps they had been carrying silently. That moment of honesty did not weaken my role. It strengthened trust. It shifted frustration into ownership. We turned the project around not because I had the answers, but because I created space for the team to find them together.

Credibility, consistency, and connection do not just build influence. They build belonging.

We changed the project trajectory not because I had all the answers, but because I created space for the team to find them together.

The Influence of Informal Leaders

Every organization has informal leaders. They do not always have a title, but they carry enormous trust. They shape culture, speak the truth without filtering it, and influence outcomes that never appear on a chart.

When I think about influence without authority, I think of Linda.

Linda was a receiving clerk. No big title. No big paycheck. But she was one of the most respected people in the entire area. She knew her work inside and out and did it with quiet excellence. She greeted everyone with warmth, made new hires feel seen, and carried herself with pride that was impossible to ignore.

A vice president once told me Linda made him feel more welcomed than any of his peers or direct reports. That is influence.

Every organization has someone like Linda. If you have not found yours yet, step out of your office and look around. These people lead with care and consistency. They are truth tellers. They are cultural compasses. And you can learn more about leadership from them than from most executive seminars.

This isn't about strategy or politics. It's about recognizing the people who lead with care and consistency, regardless of role. Learn from them. Partner with them. Let them be your truth tellers and your cultural compass.

You'll learn more about leadership from them than you will in most executive seminars. Because informal leaders like Linda remind us what leadership really looks like.

Influence Isn't Owned. It's Extended.

True leaders do not hoard influence. They lift others with it. Your job is not only to get work done. Your job is to help people rise.

Influence grows when you mentor someone who reminds you of your younger self, recommend a colleague for a stretch opportunity, amplify an overlooked idea, or step aside so someone else can lead.

Jeff, my mentor, understood this. He took a chance on me when I was young, ambitious, and probably a little too confident. He gave me projects I was not fully ready for and let me learn by doing. When I stumbled, he did not rescue me. He helped me understand what happened and what to try next.

Jeff used his influence to create space for my growth. He spent his political capital advocating for me in rooms I was not in. When I became a leader, I tried to do the same. I recommended people for promotions even when it meant losing them. I gave stretch assignments to prepare people for what was next. I took responsibility when things went wrong and shared credit when things went right.

Many of those leaders now sit in vice president, director, and even CEO roles. I am a proud "mama". I still receive notes from people I have not worked with in more than twenty years. "I thank you for everything I have become today." "I am the leader I am because of what you taught me."

My hope is that years from now, someone you led reaches out and says the same to you. That is how influence multiplies. When you lift others, they go on to lift others. The ripple carries on long after you are gone.

That's how influence multiplies. When you use yours to lift others, they go on to lift others. The ripple effect extends far beyond what you can see.

Don't Mistake Influence for Control

Great leaders do not demand compliance. They create the conditions for people to succeed. Control might feel efficient, but it burns people out. Influence takes longer, but it creates ownership. And ownership is where innovation lives.

If your team only moves when you push, you are managing. If they move because they are clear, inspired, and trusted, then you are leading.

I learned this distinction while working with a manufacturing team struggling with quality issues. The plant manager, Robert, tried to solve the problems through more oversight, more checklists, and more rules. Defects kept happening.

"What if we tried something different?" I asked. "What if instead of controlling the process, we helped people own it?"

Robert was skeptical, but he agreed to try. We brought the team together and asked two simple questions: "What would it take for you to feel proud of every product that leaves this line?" and "What do we need to do differently to make that happen?"

The conversation that followed was eye-opening. The team identified root causes Robert had not seen. They suggested improvements he had not considered. They volunteered to take ownership of quality far beyond any checklist.

Within three months, defect rates dropped by 35 percent. Not because of more control, but because of more ownership.

Robert told me later, "I thought leadership meant having all the answers. I learned it means asking the right questions and trusting people to find the answers."

Your Leadership Credit Score

Every interaction with your team either builds trust or erodes it. There's no neutral ground.

Trust builders:

- Following through on what you say you'll do.
- Admitting when you're wrong or don't know something.
- Taking responsibility when things go sideways.
- Giving credit where it's due.
- Showing up the same way, especially under pressure.

Trust breakers:

- Making promises you can't keep.
- Taking credit for work that isn't yours.
- Throwing others under the bus when things get messy.
- Being unpredictable under stress.

- Saying one thing in meetings and doing another in practice.

I worked with a leader named Carlos who was bleeding trust without realizing it. Carlos was smart, hardworking, and genuinely cared about results. But he had developed a dangerous habit: he said yes to everything.

New deadline that seemed impossible? "Absolutely, we'll make it work."

Additional resources the team desperately needed? "I'll get those for you by Friday."

Process changes that would require complete system overhauls? "Sure, no problem."

Carlos thought he was being supportive and solution oriented. His team saw someone they couldn't count on. When this pattern finally came to light, Carlos was stunned. "But I'm always trying to help," he said. "I never want to let anyone down." "That's exactly the problem," I told him. "When you say yes to everything, your yes means nothing."

The turnaround wasn't dramatic or fast. Carlos started small: making promises he could keep. He would say "let me look into that and get back to you" instead of giving instant agreement. He chose to be honest about real constraints instead of painting rosy pictures.

It took months, but Carlos rebuilt his credibility one kept promise at a time. And when people finally knew they could count on his word, his influence grew exponentially.

The Power of Presence

Want to expand your influence today? Start with presence.

Presence is deceptively simple. It means you stop multitasking. You stop rehearsing your response while someone else is still talking. You make eye contact. You listen without rushing to fix.

When you practice presence, three things happen:

- Trust deepens. People share sooner and more honestly when they feel they are being heard.

- Clarity improves. You catch the nuance behind words, tone, and body language instead of missing signals.

- Engagement rises. People bring their ideas forward because they know they will be taken seriously.

Think about your own experience. Have you ever walked away from a conversation feeling truly heard? Chances are it wasn't the solution that stayed with you, it was the attention. Presence sends a powerful message: *"I see you. I value you. You matter."*

Presence is not only important one-on-one, but also with the group. In group settings, it shapes dynamics in ways leaders often underestimate. In meetings, presence means scanning the room for voices that are holding back, noticing when someone is interrupted, or pausing long enough for quieter contributors to step in. Influence often comes from creating conditions where every perspective can surface.

Here's a practical reset to try: the next time you are in conversation, put aside devices, slow your breathing, and commit to listening until the other person is fully finished. Notice what shifts when silence is allowed to stretch instead of being filled.

Influence doesn't come from being the smartest voice in the room. It comes from being the most attentive one. When your leadership creates the conditions for others to feel seen and safe, you won't have to chase influence. You'll already have it.

The Influence of Authentic Vulnerability

There's a difference between vulnerability and oversharing. Authentic vulnerability is intentional. It's about showing your humanity in service of connection and growth.

I saw the power of this during a difficult merger. Uncertainty was high, people were worried about their jobs, and morale was at an all-time low.

In one team meeting, I could have leaned on the usual corporate script: "Stay focused, things will work out." Instead, I chose honesty.

"I don't have all the answers about what this merger means for us," I said. "I'm concerned about some of the same things you are. But I can promise this: I'll share information as soon as I have it. I'll fight for this team every chance I get. And we'll figure it out together."

The room went silent at first. Then questions came. Concerns surfaced. The conversation turned real.

That moment didn't make me look weak. It made me human. And it gave others permission to be human too.

Months later, when the dust had settled, several teammates told me that conversation was the turning point. Not because I had the answers, but because I was honest about not having them.

Authentic vulnerability doesn't diminish your influence. It multiplies it.

The Multiplier Effect

The most influential leaders don't just get things done. They multiply the capabilities of everyone around them.

I worked with a leader named Jay who embodied this principle. Jay had inherited a struggling sales team. Previous leaders had tried everything: new incentive plans, additional training, performance improvement programs. Nothing worked.

Jay took a different approach. Instead of focusing on what the team was doing wrong, he focused on what each person did well. He spent time understanding their individual strengths, motivations, and career aspirations.

For one team member who was great at building relationships but struggled with closing, Jay paired her with a mentor who could help with closing techniques. For another who was analytical but shy, he created opportunities to present to smaller, internal groups to build confidence.

Jay didn't try to make everyone the same. He helped everyone become their best version of themselves.

Within a year, the team went from worst-performing to top-performing.

That's the multiplier effect. *When you develop people's capabilities instead of just managing their outputs, you create leaders who go on to create more leaders.*

Jay's influence extended far beyond his own team because he invested in people's potential, not just their performance.

Your Turn: Tools to Grow Influence and Expand Impact

Let's get tactical. Here's how you build real, lasting influence.

Tool 13: Leadership Credibility Builder

Purpose: To strengthen your leadership presence and trustworthiness.

Instructions: Reflect on the following:

- Competence: What do I consistently do well that my team or peers rely on?

- Consistency: Where do I show up dependably? Where am I unpredictable?

- Connection: When was the last time I really listened without interrupting or problem-solving?

Action: Choose one area to elevate this week and communicate it out loud.

Ex: "I've realized I've been a bit reactive lately. I'm working on slowing down and listening better."

Credibility isn't built in silence. Let people see your growth.

Mirror Move: Choose one person whose respect would expand your influence (a peer, informal leader, or stakeholder). Share your credibility commitment with them directly: "I'm working on being more consistent with follow-through. I'd value your perspective on how I'm doing." Ask them to hold you accountable. When you build credibility with influential people transparently, they become advocates for your growth.

Tool 14: The Influence Audit

Purpose: To assess your current influence and identify areas for growth.

Instructions: Rate yourself (1-10) on each element of influence:

- Credibility: People trust my judgment and follow-through

- Consistency: I show up steadily, especially under pressure

- Connection: I make people feel seen, heard, and valued

- Authenticity: I'm genuine and honest in my interactions
- Generosity: I use my influence to lift others up
- Presence: I'm fully engaged when interacting with others

For areas scoring below 8, ask:

- What specific behaviors are limiting my influence here?
- What's one action I can take this week to improve?
- Who could I ask for feedback on this area?

Mirror Move: Pick your lowest scoring area and ask three people from different parts of your network (boss, peer, team member) for specific feedback on that area. Then report back to all three on what you learned and what you're changing. This transparent approach to growth builds credibility across your influence network.

Tool 15: The Multiplier Assessment

Purpose: To evaluate how well you're developing others and expanding collective capability.

Instructions: Think about your direct reports or key team members. For each person, ask:

- Do they perform better because of my leadership?
- Am I helping them develop skills they didn't have before?
- Are they taking on more responsibility and ownership?
- Do they feel more confident and capable?
- Are they ready for bigger challenges?

If you answered "no" to more than half of these questions for anyone, that's your development priority.

Action: Choose one person and commit to having a development conversation this week. Ask them:

- What skills do you want to build?
- What challenges do you want to take on?
- How can I better support your growth?

Mirror Move: Choose one person you identified as a development priority and take a deliberate step to multiply their capability this week. This could be delegating a meaningful responsibility, offering targeted coaching, or giving them space to lead a conversation or decision. Your goal is simple. Create one intentional moment that helps them grow beyond where they are today.

Tool 16: Strategic Influence Mapping

Purpose: To help you identify, prioritize, and engage key relationships that can amplify your influence and expand your leadership reach, intentionally and consistently.

Instructions: This month, you will map your influence landscape and take deliberate actions to strengthen your most strategic relationships.

Step 1: Identify Your Influence Circle

List five people in your organization or network who meet at least one of the following criteria:

- They are informal leaders with wide respect and reach.
- They challenge and sharpen your thinking.

- They have access, perspective, or authority you don't.

- They are culture shapers whom others naturally follow.

These can include peers, stakeholders, mentors, emerging leaders, or cross-functional allies.

Create a matrix with these headings and then rate the relationship.

Name | How this relationship could be mutually beneficial | Current strength of relationship (1-5)

Step 2: Choose Your Top Three

Pick the three people where you see the most opportunity for mutual growth or collaboration.

For each, answer:

- What do I want to learn, build, or co-create with this person?

- What value or insight can I offer them?

- What intentional action will I take to build trust?

Name:	What you want to learn/build.	What you will offer.	Action you'll take this week.

Step 3: Take Action and Track Progress

Over the next four weeks, take one intentional action per week for each person. Actions could include:

- Sharing an idea or resource

- Offering support on a project

- Inviting them to coffee or a walk-and-talk
- Giving authentic, unsolicited recognition
- Asking for their insight regarding a strategic challenge

Log your actions and reflect each week:

- What changed in the relationship?
- What new opportunities opened up?
- How did this impact your influence or credibility?

Mirror Move: At the end of the month, reflect with a peer, coach, or manager:

- What did you learn about how influence really works in your organization?
- How did you grow through these intentional connections?
- What relationships do you want to keep investing in and why?

Final Thoughts: Lead Beyond Yourself

Influence, at its best, is never about addition. It is about multiplication. This chapter has opened the fourth pillar, Expanding Influence and Impact, by focusing on how you build real influence through trust, presence, and generosity.

You do not need a promotion or permission to lead with influence. You simply need to decide that you will.

The leaders who make the greatest impact are not the ones collecting followers. They are the ones multiplying leadership in others. And that is the difference that matters most — not how many people looked to you, but how many learned to lead because of you.

The most powerful thing you will ever do is not what happens in the room when you are present. It is what continues long after you have left it.

Before you move on, pause and consider:

When you step out of the room, what remains because you were there?

CHAPTER SIX

When the Mirror Cracks

Leadership Will Challenge You!

After watching leaders like Laura transform their cultures and build genuine influence, you might think the path forward is straightforward. Just follow the tools, model the behaviors, and watch your leadership flourish.

I wish it were that simple.

Leadership isn't all reflection tools, feedback loops, and influence building. Sometimes, leadership just hurts.

Sometimes, you pour your energy into people, and they are disappointed anyway. Sometimes, you take the high road and still get steamrolled. Sometimes, you lead with clarity and integrity, and the outcome is still a mess.

Leadership will stretch you. It will break you open. It will bring you to your knees. And when that happens, the question isn't "How do I avoid this?"

As you move deeper into the fourth pillar of The Leadership Mirror Framework, Expanding Influence and Impact, this chapter explores what happens when things break, and how your response in those moments can strengthen your influence and deepen your impact.

You're Going to Get It Wrong

You'll miss the signs. You'll overreact. You'll hold on too long. Or not long enough. You'll try to fix things that aren't yours to fix. You'll let someone down, even when your intentions were good.

And in those moments, when the mirror cracks and you don't like what's staring back at you, you'll be tempted to look away.

Don't.

Those cracks aren't the end of your leadership. They're the beginning of your growth.

Every leader I've worked with has a moment that humbles them completely. The project that fails despite their best efforts. The team member who quits unexpectedly. The decision seemed right but created unintended consequences. The feedback that stings because it's true.

These moments don't mean you're a bad leader. They mean you're human.

The leaders who thrive aren't the ones who avoid mistakes. They're the ones who face them head on. They look at what went wrong, own their part in it, and use that knowledge to lead better next time.

Sustainable leadership is about progression. It's about showing up, learning, and trying again with more wisdom than you had before.

The mirror will crack. That's guaranteed. But what you do next, how you respond, how you grow, how you lead through the difficulty, that's where your character shows.

Failure Doesn't Disqualify You. Denial Does.

You are not expected to be perfect. You are expected to take responsibility.

This is where many leaders get stuck. They either collapse into shame or push the blame onto others. They defend. They disappear. Or they double down on the same behavior that caused the damage in the first place.

It is not failure that breaks trust. It is the refusal to own it.

There is a better way. Own what happened. Repair what you can. Learn what you need to. Then lead forward with scar tissue and wisdom.

The most powerful leadership moment you will ever have is not when everything is going well. It is when it is not, and your team watches how you respond.

The Cost of Leading in a Culture Built on Fear

I was part of a high-stakes project with intense pressure from the top. The expectations were impossible, deadlines were unrealistic, and the leadership culture was driven by fear rather than clarity.

One day, our senior leader called us into a meeting. The room felt heavy before he even walked in. When he finally entered, he slammed a notebook onto the table and went straight into a tirade. He berated people by name. He questioned our competence. His voice never rose to shouting, but the intensity was sharp enough to cut the air in half.

I remember sitting there feeling a mixture of anger, embarrassment, and disbelief. Not because I had never worked under pressure before, but because in that moment I saw how fear changes people. The team shut down. No one asked questions. No one clarified expectations. No one dared to share the truth about the barriers we were facing.

We left that meeting more exhausted than we had been when we walked in. Not because of the workload, but because of the emotional weight of being humiliated in front of our peers.

That day, something cracked for me. I realized that fear-based leadership does not produce excellence. It produces compliance. It produces silence. It produces people who are technically present but emotionally checked out.

What surprised me most was how quickly the effects spread. Within hours, side conversations began. People vented quietly in hallways. Others withdrew completely. Collaboration stalled because no one wanted to set off the next emotional explosion.

I carried that experience for a long time. Not because of the leader's behavior, but because it forced me to confront something in myself. It made me ask, *What is it like when I am under pressure? What version of me do people experience when I am stressed, afraid, or trying to prove myself?*

That moment reminded me that leadership cracks do not always show up as big mistakes or dramatic failures. Sometimes the crack is the emotional ripple we create without even realizing it. And if we are not careful, that ripple becomes the culture people work in every day.

You do not need to be flawless. It's better to be real. Your team needs to see what accountability, humility, and grace look like in action.

That is the kind of leadership people remember.

The Hidden Cost of Leadership Shame

Maria, a director, was struggling with a team that had lost trust in her leadership.

Six months earlier, Maria decided to restructure her department without involving her team in the process. She believed she was protecting them from unnecessary stress by handling the details herself. Instead, they felt blindsided and devalued.

When the restructuring did not go as planned and two strong performers quit, Maria spiraled into shame. She started avoiding her team. Meetings became infrequent. When people asked questions, she grew defensive.

"I feel like a fraud," she told me. "Maybe I am not cut out for leadership."

That was when I introduced her to Dr. Brené Brown's research on shame resilience. Brown's work shows that shame thrives in secrecy, silence, and judgment, but it cannot survive empathy, vulnerability, and connection. As she writes, "If we can share our story with someone who responds with empathy and understanding, shame cannot survive."

The antidote to leadership shame is not perfection. It is courage.

Maria began having honest conversations with her team about what went wrong. She acknowledged the impact of her choices and asked for their feedback on how to rebuild trust.

It was not easy. Some conversations were tense. Others were quiet. But over time, something shifted. Her team began to see her effort, not just her mistakes.

Six months later, their engagement scores were among the highest in the division. Not because Maria stopped making mistakes, but because she learned to lead through them with honesty and grace.

If you have ever felt like you let people down, you know that shame can convince you that you are unworthy of leading. But repair begins the moment you choose courage over silence.

Your Relationship with Discomfort Defines Your Growth

We love leadership when we feel in control. But real growth? That happens in discomfort.

Discomfort reveals:

- What you truly value.

- How emotionally mature you are.

- Whether you are willing to adapt.

- If you stay grounded in uncertainty.

Avoid discomfort and you shrink. Move through it, and you expand.

I have watched leaders face budget cuts that forced them to make impossible choices. I've seen them navigate team conflicts that had no clean solutions. I've witnessed them making decisions with incomplete information while everyone waited for answers they didn't have.

The leaders who grew from these experiences didn't avoid the discomfort. They leaned into it. They asked hard questions. They had difficult conversations. They stayed present even when every instinct told them to retreat.

You don't need to be fearless to lead well. You need to be honest. And brave enough to stay in discomfort long enough to learn from it.

Growth lives there.

Repair Is a Leadership Skill

Let's say this plainly: you will hurt people.

Not because you're a bad person. Not because you're careless. But because leadership involves power. And power, even when exercised with the best of intentions, can create harm.

The question isn't whether you'll get it wrong. You will. The real question is whether you're willing to own it and repair it.

One repair conversation I witnessed reshaped my client Noah's entire view of leadership accountability.

Noah had been leading a project team preparing for a major client presentation. One of his team members, David, had prepared a section that Noah thought needed significant changes. Instead of giving him constructive feedback privately, he decided to "workshop" David's content in front of the entire team.

Noah thought this approach was collaborative feedback; however, David experienced it as public humiliation.

Noah didn't realize the impact until a colleague pulled him aside later and said, "You need to know that David is really upset. He feels like you threw him under the bus in there."

Noah's first instinct was to defend himself. When he told me about it in our coaching session, he said, "I was just trying to make the presentation better. He was being too sensitive."

"How do you think you would have felt if someone had done that to you?" I asked him.

He paused. "I would have been mortified," he admitted. "I realize that my intent didn't matter if the impact was harmful."

I encouraged Noah to have a conversation with David. Not to explain himself, but to listen.

"David," he said when they met, "I've heard that our meeting didn't feel good for you. Can you help me understand what happened from your perspective?"

David was quiet for a moment. Then he said, "I worked really hard on that section. When you started picking it apart in front of everyone, it felt like you were saying my work wasn't good enough. And that I wasn't good enough."

When Noah shared this with me later, he said, "That hit me like a physical blow. Because I did think his work was good. I just wanted to make it great. But my delivery completely undermined that message."

Noah apologized. Not a defensive apology that tried to explain his intentions, but a real one that acknowledged David's experience. He told David what he would do differently next time and asked what David needed from him to move forward.

David appreciated the conversation. But more importantly, it changed how Noah gave feedback. He learned that public feedback should be about celebrating and reinforcing good work. Developmental feedback should happen privately, with care and respect for the person's dignity.

Repair is one of most overlooked responsibilities in leadership. It requires presence, humility, and the courage to step into discomfort without defensiveness.

Repair doesn't erase what happened. But it opens the door to trust again. It creates a chance for people to feel seen, heard, and respected even in the aftermath of a misstep.

When you don't address harm, your team will find ways to protect themselves. They'll withdraw. They'll stop speaking up. They'll nod in agreement but disengage quietly. Unrepaired harm doesn't vanish; it settles into the culture.

If you care about your people and performance, then you must care about repair. It's not a side note to leadership. It is leadership.

The REPAIR Framework: Leading Through the Cracks

Every leader will eventually face a moment when the mirror cracks. Something goes wrong. A relationship breaks down. A decision causes unintended pain.

Repair is not about perfection. It is about progression. It is a skill that can be practiced and strengthened like any other.

Here is the model I teach leaders who want to rebuild trust after a setback:

R – **Recognize** what happened and your role in it.

E – **Empathize** with how others experienced it.

P – **Pause** before defending or explaining.

A – **Act** to make things right.

I – **Integrate** what you learned into new habits.

R – **Reconnect** through trust and consistent behavior.

This is how you lead through the cracks instead of around them. It begins inward with reflection, then extends outward through reconnection.

When you can do that, your leadership becomes not just effective but human.

When Your Team Loses Faith

Sometimes, the mirror doesn't just crack. It shatters completely.

I worked with a leader named Sam whose team had completely lost confidence in his leadership after a series of broken promises. Sam's first instinct was to try to win people back with public gestures and new initiatives. But trust isn't rebuilt with speeches or strategy sessions.

We started with what Sam called "the apology tour." Individual conversations with each team member where he acknowledged his mistakes, listened to their concerns, and asked what he could do to earn back their trust.

Some people weren't ready to hear it. Others were willing to give him another chance if he proved he would change.

Sam did not try to fix everything at once. He focused on reliability. Every commitment, no matter how small, was kept. He asked for feedback regularly and acted on it. He admitted when he did not know something instead of pretending he had all the answers.

It took almost a year for the culture to shift. Not everyone stayed, but those who did became some of his strongest advocates. They had watched him do the hard work of rebuilding.

Sam followed every step of the REPAIR process. He recognized what had gone wrong, empathized with his team, paused before defending, acted on their feedback, integrated what he learned, and reconnected through consistent follow-through.

Sometimes you must break completely before you can rebuild. And sometimes, that is exactly what you need.

The Compound Effect of Resilient Leadership

When you consistently lead through challenges with honesty, humility, and courage, here's what happens:

- Week 1: You feel the relief of being authentic instead of perfect.

- Month 1: Your team starts bringing you problems earlier because they trust you to handle them well.

- Month 3: Others begin coming to you for advice when they're struggling.

- Month 6: You develop a reputation as someone who can be trusted in crisis.

- Year 1: You become the leader others want to learn from and work with

- Year 2: Your influence grows because people know you've been tested and proven yourself.

This is not about seeking out failure or drama. It is about recognizing that the way you handle inevitable challenges defines who you become as a leader.

Each time you practice repair, you build resilience. Each time you take responsibility, you strengthen trust. Each time you model courage, you invite others to do the same.

Resilient leadership is not built overnight. It is built moment by moment, choice by choice, conversation by conversation.

Look inward to learn. Lead outward to heal.

Your Turn: Tools to Lead Through the Cracks

Every leader faces moments when things fall apart. When that happens, reflection without repair keeps you stuck. Repair without reflection repeats the pattern. The goal is both. These tools are designed to help you reflect, repair, and rise without slipping into shame or defensiveness.

Tool 17: From Failure to Forward Movement

Purpose: To transform leadership setbacks into growth and action

Instructions:

1. Name it clearly: Write one sentence describing what went wrong (no spin, no blame).

2. Own your part: What did you do or not do that contributed to the outcome?

3. Reflect with purpose: What are you most proud of, even in the mess? Would you do differently?

4. Identify repairs needed: Who was impacted and needs to hear from you?

5. Take visible action: Choose one recent mistake. Work through all five steps. Share your visible action with your team within 48 hours.

Mirror Move: The Team Reckoning. Choose a mistake that affected your whole team. Call a team meeting with one agenda item: "taking responsibility".

Say: "I want to talk about [situation] and own my part in what went wrong." Walk through steps 1-4 publicly, then ask: "What's one change you'd like to see me make to rebuild your trust?"

Write down every suggestion without defending yourself. Pick one and implement it within a week. Report back to the team.

The uncomfortable part? Your team has opinions about your leadership you may not want to hear. They'll suggest changes that challenge your ego. Do it anyway.

Tool 18: The Repair Conversation Framework

Purpose: To guide you through difficult conversations when you need to make things right.

Instructions: Before the conversation:

- Get clear on what you want to acknowledge.

- Focus on impact, not just intent.

- Prepare to listen without defending.

During the conversation:

- Start with: "I realize that [situation] may not have felt good for you. Can you help me understand your experience?"

- Listen completely before responding.

- Acknowledge their experience: "I can see how that would feel [frustrating/dismissive/uncomfortable/etc.]"

- Take responsibility: "That's not the impact I wanted to have, and I take responsibility for my part."

- Ask: "What do you need from me to move forward?"

After the conversation:

- Follow through on any commitments you made.

- Check in again within two weeks.

- Make consistent and visible changes in your behavior.

Mirror Move: Identify the one person you've been avoiding having a repair conversation with. The one where you think: *It's probably fine* or *They've moved on* or *It would just make things weird*.

That's the conversation you're having this week.

Use the framework exactly as written but add this challenge: after they tell you their experience, sit in silence for 10 full seconds before responding. Count them: one-Mississippi, two-Mississippi. Then reflect what you heard before you say anything else.

At the end of the conversation, ask: "Is there anything else I should know about how this affected you?" Even if you think you've covered everything.

The uncomfortable part? You might discover that something you thought was minor was significant to them. You might learn that your leadership impact is different than your leadership intent. You might realize you've been wrong about how "fine" things are with them.

Tool 19: Reality Check and Reframe

Purpose: To shift from shame spirals to learning and growth.

Instructions:

When facing a leadership setback, reframe your thoughts:

- Instead of *I'm a terrible leader* → *What can I learn from this?*

- Instead of *Everyone thinks I'm incompetent* → *What feedback would help me improve?*

- Instead of *I always mess things up* → *What specific behavior can I change?*

- Instead of *This defines who I am* → *This is one moment in my leadership journey.*

Mirror Move: The External Reality Check

Pick one reframing question and test it with someone who witnessed your setback. Instead of just thinking through it yourself, ask them directly.

"I'm trying to learn from what happened. From your perspective, what should I pay attention to?" or "If you were coaching me through this, what behavior would you suggest I work on?"

Make it clear you want honest input, not reassurance: "I'm not looking for you to make me feel better. I'm looking for real insight."

The uncomfortable part? Their feedback might be harder to hear than your self-reflection. They might point out blind spots you don't see. They might be more direct than you expect. Thank them and resist explaining yourself.

Final Thoughts: You Are Still the Person in the Mirror

When things fall apart, when trust erodes, when the project fails or the team fractures, it is easy to question everything. Especially yourself.

But remember this: the person looking back at you is still there. Maybe bruised, maybe tired, but still capable, still growing, still leading.

Your people will look to you for how to respond when things go wrong. When you lead through repair with honesty, humility, and grace, you show them what resilience really looks like.

Great leaders do not avoid the cracks. They learn to lead through them. The cracks do not destroy your reflection. They deepen it.

- Your scars become credentials.
- Your failures become curriculum.
- Your repairs become reputation.

This, too, is Expanding Influence and Impact. Your greatest impact does not come from the seasons when everything is smooth, but from how you show up when the mirror cracks, when trust has to be rebuilt, and when people are watching to see whether you live what you teach.

Look inward. Lead outward. And keep repairing. That is what real leadership looks like.

CHAPTER SEVEN

The Leadership Legacy

How you lead becomes what you leave behind.

After everything we've explored - looking in the mirror, reclaiming your energy, designing culture, growing influence, and leading through the cracks - you might think the work is done. But there's one more conversation to have. One that many leaders avoid.

Legacy.

We talk about it like it's something that happens at the end, after the retirement party, the gold watch, and the final email that says, "Thanks and best of luck."

Your leadership legacy isn't built someday. It's being built right now.

Every conversation. Every decision. Every "I've got your back." Every "Not today, we don't treat people like that here." Every "I'm sorry, I missed the mark."

It all adds up.

Your legacy isn't a single speech. It's a pattern. A ripple that begins long before anyone calls it a legacy.

By the time you reach this chapter, you are deep into the fourth pillar of The Leadership Mirror Framework, Expanding Influence and Impact. You have learned how your presence shapes culture and how your behavior builds trust. Now we bring it all together in the most practical way of all: the legacy you are creating in real time through the people you lead and the patterns you leave behind.

And while intention matters, it's not enough. Legacy isn't what you *intend* to leave. It's what you *live* every day, through how you show up and how others experience you.

What Will People Say When You're Not in the Room?

This isn't about gossip or office politics. It's about presence and perception.

When your name comes up, how do people feel? When you leave a meeting, what energy lingers in the room? When someone new joins your team, what do they learn about your values without you ever saying a word?

I'll never forget the day I heard two team members talking about me. One of them called me a "bitch."

Holy cow. That was a punch in the gut. I thought I was protecting them from the "stuff" rolling downhill, but that wasn't how they saw it. Somewhere along the way, my good intentions had turned into pressure they couldn't carry.

I was being pulled in too many directions, and without realizing it, I was doing the same to them. Exhausted. Frustrated. Overwhelmed.

Instead of walking away and letting the comment fester, I chose to face it head-on. I asked them about what I'd heard. You should have seen their faces when they realized I knew.

I told them the words hurt and not just because they were blunt, but because they described a version of me I didn't want to become. I wanted to be someone they could trust, not fear.

That moment turned out to be a turning point. We had some honest, uncomfortable, and ultimately powerful discussions. From that, we made a few commitments:

- We agreed to be more open and honest. Trust goes both ways.

- We wouldn't let issues fester. Even when the truth stung, we'd speak it.

- If there was a problem, they'd come to me directly. No side chatter, no rumors.

That day was hard. But instead of avoiding discomfort, I leaned into it. I'm glad I did. It didn't just change how we worked; it changed how we related to each other.

Your legacy is built in the moments you think no one's noticing, and in how you respond when everyone is.

What I learned that day was this: reputation is what people think about you when you're in the room. Legacy is what they say about you when you're not.

The difference between the two isn't your title or your accomplishments. It's how you make people feel.

You Don't Need a Perfect Run, You Need a Pattern

Legacy isn't about a flawless record. You will make mistakes. You've probably made some already.

What matters most isn't perfection. It's pattern.

- Do people know what to expect from you?

- Do they experience consistency, care, and clarity even when things are hard?

- Do you follow through, even when no one's watching?

Over time, those small, repeatable choices form your impact. And your impact becomes your legacy.

It's not built in big displays, but in how you show up when it would be easier not to.

That is what "lived intention" really means. It's what people experience because of you, not what you hope they will someday remember.

Your leadership legacy is written in a thousand quiet choices. The ones that show your character when no one is keeping score. The ones that remind people they can count on you, even in uncertainty.

Your pattern is your proof. And your pattern becomes your story.

The Invisible Threads

Patterns don't end with you. They echo in the people who follow.

Every leader leaves invisible threads behind. They show up in what others learn from you, copy from you, or carry forward because of you.

That sarcastic remark you made about a senior leader in front of your team gave them permission to gossip. That time you skipped the hard conversation taught them that avoiding conflict is easier than accountability. That moment you took ownership for a mistake no one else knew about modeled integrity.

The people you lead are weaving your example into their own leadership DNA. Even the parts you didn't mean to teach.

I saw this lesson unfold while coaching a leadership team whose CEO, Michael, had a habit of checking his phone during meetings. He wasn't rude or disengaged. Just busy, trying to stay on top of everything.

But within three months, every leader on his team was doing the same thing. Each one had absorbed his behavior without realizing it. Meetings became distracted, decisions dragged, and the team's attention scattered.

When I pointed it out, Michael was shocked. "I had no idea they were watching that closely."

"They always are," I told him. "Especially when you think they're not."

From that day forward, Michael started putting his phone face down in every meeting. He made eye contact. He asked follow-up questions. He was fully present.

Within weeks, his team followed his lead. The quality of discussion improved. Decisions came faster. People felt heard again.

That is the invisible thread of legacy. Your behaviors become their behaviors. Your values become their values. Your patterns become their patterns.

Your legacy doesn't just affect today. It shapes how the next leader leads, because of you or in spite of you.

That's why self-awareness isn't optional. It's a responsibility.

The Ripple Effect of Recognition

Some leaders chase visibility. Others create it for those around them.

Maria was a manufacturing supervisor who understood legacy in a way that changed an entire organization. She worked the night shift at a chemical plant. It wasn't glamorous work or high visibility, but Maria saw something others missed: every person on her shift mattered.

She started small. She learned everyone's names within her first week. She found out who had kids, who was taking classes, and who was facing challenges at home.

Then she began a simple practice. Each week, Maria wrote one handwritten note to recognize someone's contribution. Not for the big wins everyone already noticed, but for the small acts that made a difference: the extra care, the quiet consistency, the willingness to help a teammate.

"Miguel, I noticed how you helped train the new guy this week without being asked. That kind of teamwork makes this place better." "Shanaya, your attention to detail caught that quality issue before it became a problem. Thank you for caring."

Those notes started appearing on lockers. People took photos of them. They shared them with their families.

Before long, other supervisors noticed the energy on Maria's shift. People were more engaged. Quality improved. Absenteeism dropped.

Within a year, the plant manager asked Maria to share her approach with others. Within two years, the entire plant had adopted a recognition culture modeled after her simple act of appreciation.

Five years later, when Maria retired, the company had redesigned its formal recognition program based on what she started.

That's legacy. One person, one consistent practice, rippling outward to change hundreds of lives.

Maria didn't set out to transform a company. She simply chose to see people and let them know they mattered.

That's what "lived intention" looks like. It's leadership practiced, not promised.

You can do it too. Legacy is built in the smallest actions repeated with purpose. The kind that remind people they matter long before anyone puts it in writing.

You Are Already Someone's Leadership Role Model

You may not realize it, but someone is watching you.

They're taking mental notes. They're learning what leadership looks like from how you show up every day.

How does that make you feel? Proud? Nervous? Maybe both.

It might be your team. It might be a peer. It might be your child, quietly observing how you walk through the door after a hard day.

Legacy isn't built through what you say about leadership. It's built through what people feel after experiencing your leadership.

I think about my former mentee, Jessica. She was disciplined and driven, but she struggled to give difficult feedback. She would wait too long to have hard conversations, hoping things would work themselves out.

Together, we worked on having direct and compassionate conversations. I showed her how to be both honest and kind, how to lead with clarity and care at the same time.

Years later, Jessica called me from her new role as a regional director. "I wanted to thank you," she said. "Not just for the coaching, but for showing me what courageous leadership looks like. I just had the hardest conversation of my career, and I handled it the way you taught me - directly and with dignity."

She went on to tell me that she was now mentoring three other leaders using the same approach, and that one of them had just been promoted and was teaching it to her team.

That's how legacy multiplies. Through the people you develop, who go on to develop others, who go on to develop others.

You don't have to have a big title or years of experience to make that kind of difference. You just have to live your intention and let people see what integrity looks like in real time.

If you want to multiply your impact the same way, you'll find a tool called *The Mentorship Map* at the end of this chapter to help you begin.

The Best Legacies Are Lived, Not Left

When most people hear the word "legacy," they think "later." But legacy doesn't happen someday. It happens now.

Here's what that looks like:

- Saying the hard truth with love
- Investing in people, not just performance
- Choosing principles over popularity
- Building systems that outlast you
- Helping others grow into leaders, not just doers

That last one. That's the magic. *Legacy isn't about you. It's about what you help others become.*

If you're not growing leaders, then you're not leading.

I learned this from watching my former boss, Patricia. She could have hoarded opportunities, information, and credit. Instead, she used her position to elevate others.

When there was a high-visibility project, she asked, "Who on my team needs this experience?" When there was a speaking opportunity, she recommended someone else. When senior leadership asked for her opinion, she often said, "Let me bring in the person who's closest to this work."

Patricia wasn't diminishing herself. She was multiplying her impact.

Five years after she left that role, four of her former direct reports were in senior leadership positions across different companies.

Each of them credited Patricia with showing them that leadership is about lifting others up, not climbing over them.

That is what lived legacy looks like. It begins in small, intentional choices that build people, not egos.

And it starts long before anyone gives you credit for it.

The Compound Effect of Small Gestures

Sometimes legacy is built in moments that seem insignificant at the time.

I worked with a leader named Thuli who made a quiet habit of staying late on Friday afternoons. Not to catch up on email or review reports, but simply to be available for anyone who wanted to talk. Not always about work - sometimes about life, family, or what was weighing on them.

Most Fridays, no one stopped by. But every so often, someone would knock on her door. Maybe they were wrestling with a tough decision. Maybe they needed career advice. Maybe they just needed someone to listen.

Thuli never tracked these conversations or turned them into a program. She never mentioned them to her boss. She just kept showing up.

Years later, when Thuli moved to a different company, her team threw her a farewell party. One by one, people stood to share what her leadership had meant to them.

Their stories weren't about strategic wins or financial results. They were about those quiet Friday afternoons.

One person said, "You taught me that real leadership isn't about being important. It's about making others feel important." Another added, "I'm a better leader today because you showed me that being available matters more than being busy."

Thuli's simple practice had rippled through her entire team. Several of them had started doing the same thing with their own teams.

That's how legacy works. It doesn't depend on titles or grand gestures. It grows from the steady rhythm of care, presence, and follow-through.

Small gestures, lived consistently, can shape a culture more powerfully than any initiative or speech.

The Dark Side of Legacy

Every leader leaves a legacy, but not every legacy is one to be proud of.

Some legacies are rooted in fear. People still flinch when certain names are mentioned.

Some are marked by cynicism. Years later, people still say, "Why bother? Leadership never really cared."

Others are defined by mediocrity. Standards slipped, and "good enough" became the culture.

The truth is, legacy is not optional. The question is not whether you'll leave one, but what kind it will be.

I once attended the retirement celebration of an executive named Robert. During the reception afterward, he stood beside me with a drink in his hand and said quietly, "I wonder if I made anyone's life better, or if I just made everyone's life harder."

His words stopped me.

Robert had been highly competent. He hit his numbers, met his targets, and climbed the ladder. But he did it by burning through people, creating stress, and putting results above relationships.

As he reflected on his thirty-year career, he struggled to name a single person who was better off for having worked with him. Sadly, I couldn't disagree with him.

That is a painful legacy. And it's preventable.

The difference between a positive legacy and a negative one isn't talent or intelligence. It's intention that's lived, not just written.

Every leader has moments when they realize their pattern needs to change. I think of another executive, Evelyn, who had a reputation for being sharp but dismissive. She once told me, "I didn't mean to make people afraid of me. I just wanted them to respect me."

When she learned that her team hesitated to share ideas, she decided to change her approach. She began each meeting by asking one person to share something they had learned recently, about the business, a process, or themselves as a leader. It reminded everyone that growth, not perfection, was the goal.

Within months, the tone of her meetings shifted. People spoke up. Energy returned. Her team began to trust her again.

Evelyn's shift didn't erase the past, but it rewrote her pattern. And that's what legacy really is: a pattern of how people experience you over time.

The question isn't whether you'll leave a legacy. You will. The question is whether you'll choose to make that legacy one of fear, fatigue, or growth.

Every day gives you another chance to decide which one it will be.

Your Turn: Tools to Live and Leave Your Legacy

Legacy is not something you build later. It is something you live now. These tools help you bring intention, alignment, and daily action to the legacy you are already creating.

Tool 20: Legacy Letter to Myself

Purpose: To clarify the kind of leader you want to be and keep that vision front and center.

Instructions: Write a letter to yourself, dated five years from now. Start with: "I'm proud of the leader I've become. Here's what I'm known for…"

Include:

- How you treat people.
- What values you're known for
- What hard things you've done well
- The impact you've had on others.

Read it regularly. Let it be your compass.

Mirror Move: Words become reality when shared.

Share your legacy letter with someone you trust, a mentor, coach, or peer. Ask them:

- "What resonates with you about this vision?"
- "Where do you see me already living this?"
- "What gaps do you notice between my vision and my current leadership?"
- "Will you help hold me accountable to this?"

Then take one specific action this week that demonstrates the leader described in your letter. Make it visible to your team and explain why it matters to you.

Tool 21: The Ripple Effect Audit

Purpose: To understand how your behaviors are influencing others.

Instructions: Observe your team for one week and note:

- What behaviors of yours are they mirroring?
- What phrases do you use do they repeat?
- How does your energy affect the room?
- What unspoken messages are you sending?

Ask yourself:

- Am I proud of what they're learning from me?
- What would I want to change?
- How can I be more intentional about what I model?

Mirror Move: Turn observation into conversation.

After completing your audit, have a team discussion:

- "I've been paying attention to our team dynamics. Here's what I've noticed..."
- "What patterns do you see in how we work together?"
- "What behaviors should we reinforce?"
- "What should we change?"
- "How can I model the leadership I want to see more of?"

Then choose one behavior to adjust, something small but visible, and talk openly about the shift you are making.

Tool 22: The Mentorship Map

Purpose: To identify opportunities to develop others and multiply your impact.

Instructions: List your team members and consider:

- What strengths do they bring?
- What growth opportunities would stretch them?

- What experiences could help them learn faster?
- Who could I connect them with to expand their perspective?
- What legacy do I want them to carry forward?

Action: Select one person to invest in this month. Schedule a development conversation focused on growth rather than performance. Offer support, feedback, and one meaningful stretch opportunity such as a project, presentation, or new responsibility that expands their skills.

Be transparent about why you are doing it. You are investing where there is curiosity and potential, not playing favorites. That is what responsible leadership looks like.

Mirror Move: Make development visible and systematic.

Choose one person from your mentorship map and take three visible actions this month:

- Have a formal development conversation where you ask: "What growth do you want that goes beyond your current role?"
- Create one specific stretch opportunity for them (a presentation, project lead role, or cross-functional assignment)
- Share their progress with others: "I want to highlight how [Name] is growing in [specific area] and the impact they're having."

Then expand the culture: Ask your team, "Who else could benefit from stretch opportunities? How can we make development a team priority, not just something I do as your leader?" Document what you learn about effective development practices and use it to refine your approach with others on your mentorship map.

Final Thoughts: Your Legacy Starts Now

Your leadership legacy is not a future milestone. It is unfolding right now in how you treat people, make decisions, and respond when things get difficult.

Every day, through every interaction, you are writing the story that others will tell about you. You are shaping a culture that will outlast your time in the role. You are developing the leaders who will carry forward what they learned from you.

The question is not whether you will leave a legacy. You will. The real question is whether it will be intentional.

- Will you lead with the end in mind?

- Will you choose to make people's lives better, not just their performance stronger?

- Will you use your influence to lift others, not just to climb higher yourself?

- Will you have the courage to become the leader you once needed?

The mirror we began with in Chapter One is still here. It reflects who you are and who you are becoming.

Now you have the tools, the awareness, and the intention to like what you see.

More importantly, you have the power to help others like what they see when they look in their own mirrors.

That is the ultimate legacy: not being remembered as a great leader but being remembered as someone who created other great leaders.

The ripples of that kind of leadership extend far beyond what you will ever see. They touch lives you may never meet, solve problems you may never witness, and create positive change long after you have moved on.

Legacy isn't where leadership ends. It's where your influence expands. The more intentionally you live your values, the more the world opens in response. That's when career growth stops being a chase and starts becoming a reflection of who you have become.

Because once you begin leading this way, something shifts. The ripple you created outward begins to ripple back. The clarity you've built, the trust you've earned, and the consistency you've shown start opening new doors. Opportunities that once seemed out of reach begin to find their way to you.

You have built a foundation that is ready to carry more impact, more recognition, and more possibility.

This is the heart of Expanding Influence and Impact. The fourth pillar of The Leadership Mirror is not about chasing a bigger platform. It is about becoming the kind of leader whose everyday actions create lasting change in people, in culture, and in the work long after you are gone.

Now it's time to see where that growth can take you.

CHAPTER EIGHT

Career Advancement Amplifies with Your Growth

You have built a legacy that will outlast you, but legacy is not the end of the story. It is the beginning of something even bigger.

When you start leading from the inside out, something remarkable happens. The clarity you have gained, the consistency you have built, and the trust you have earned begin to open new doors. The ripples you have created outward start to ripple back.

You have done the hard work. So, what is the payoff?

Think back to where you started: looking in the mirror, wrestling with your inner world, reclaiming your time and energy, designing culture with intention, building influence, and learning to lead through the cracks. You have built a foundation that is strong, intentional, and visible.

Most people talk about leadership growth. You have lived it.

You showed up, even when it was uncomfortable. You reflected, wrestled, and shifted. You challenged old patterns and took accountability. You stopped blaming the team, the system, or the calendar, and started owning your part in it all.

That is more than most leaders ever do.

But you did not do all this work just to feel better. You did it because you want more.

More impact. More recognition. More opportunity. More control over your time and your future.

And you deserve it.

This is where the fourth pillar of The Leadership Mirror Framework, Expanding Influence and Impact, becomes very real. The inner work you have done was never only about feeling better on the inside. It was about changing what becomes possible on the outside, in your career, in your choices, and in the doors that begin to open because of how you now lead.

Your Career Opens Up

When you lead with clarity, consistency, and integrity, people notice. You are no longer seen as just a doer. You are seen as a trusted voice, a culture shaper, and a multiplier.

You become the person others want in the room for the tough calls, the strategic decisions, and the opportunities that matter most.

You are on the radar now, not because you are louder, but because you are clearer.

Rachel, a director I coached, experienced this transformation firsthand. She had been in the same role for three years. Competent, reliable, but often overlooked when bigger opportunities came up. Frustrated, she began thinking about leaving the company.

"I do good work," she told me. "But nobody seems to notice."

We went back to the fundamentals. Rachel looked in the mirror and realized she had been playing it safe, avoiding difficult conversations, and waiting for permission to lead.

She began reclaiming her energy, shaping culture intentionally on her team, and building authentic influence across the organization.

Six months later, she was asked to lead a cross-functional initiative that had been struggling. Nine months after that, she was promoted to senior director. A year later, she was recruited for a vice president role at another company.

"What changed?" I asked during our final conversation.

"I stopped waiting for someone to tap me on the shoulder," she said. "I started acting like the leader I wanted to become". And eventually, everyone else started seeing it too."

That is the shift.

By looking in the mirror, the job you once doubted you were ready for now feels within reach. Others start to see it too.

That internal promotion that once seemed just out of reach becomes the next obvious step. That outside role you quietly hoped for starts to feel possible. Conversations open up. And then open doors follow.

You stop seeing yourself as part of the machinery and begin realizing you have the power to move it.

Other leaders notice the impact you are making and the changes within your team. They reach out for advice on how to do the same.

You are not just progressing in your role. You are being positioned as someone who helps shape the direction of the organization.

Your influence begins to ripple across functions, across levels, and across opportunities you might never have imagined.

You Get More Control Over Your Choices

One of the biggest wins in leadership is regaining a sense of control. You stop feeling stuck or waiting for someone else to notice your value. You begin setting the tone rather than reacting to it. Decisions come from alignment instead of fear or exhaustion. You do not just take on more, you take on the right things.

When that shift happens, people notice. They trust you with more budget, more influence, and more freedom. You become the leader who delivers results without burning out yourself or your team. Most importantly, you begin choosing your path instead of defaulting into it.

Juan, an operations manager, learned this lesson through experience. Known as the "yes" guy, he was the person everyone turned to for failing projects, crises, and impossible deadlines. On the surface, he looked successful: busy, visible, and indispensable. But underneath, he was exhausted, overwhelmed, and resentful.

"I feel like I'm running on a hamster wheel," he said. "The faster I run, the faster it spins."

Over time, Juan began to understand his energy patterns, recognize his unique value, and find the courage to make better choices. The turning point came when he was asked to take on yet another urgent project while his team was already stretched thin.

Instead of saying yes automatically, he paused. He looked at capacity, priorities, and timing. Then he said no, followed by a thoughtful alternative. He proposed a different timeline, suggested other approaches, and helped identify someone better positioned to lead it.

His boss was surprised but respected the decision. The project moved forward differently. Juan's team thrived, and six months later, he was promoted into strategic planning which is a role that required exactly the discernment he had learned to practice.

"I thought saying no would limit my opportunities," Juan reflected. "Instead, it opened the right ones."

That is the power of intentional choice. You begin to notice where your energy is best spent and where it is being wasted. You stop trying to prove your worth through busyness and start leading with purpose instead of pressure.

When Who You Are Attracts What You Want

They notice the way you handle hard conversations, the way you respond to stress, and the way you develop others.

When you lead with authenticity and intention, you attract people who want more of your approach.

Other departments see your results and start calling. Recruiters reach out. Former colleagues remember you as the leader who cared and delivered results.

You stop chasing opportunities and start choosing them.

Sofia, a marketing director, experienced this shift firsthand. She had been leading with integrity and developing her people intentionally for two years. She was not actively looking for a new role, but she had built a reputation for creating high-performing, engaged teams.

One day, she received a call from a former colleague who had joined a startup.

"We are building our leadership team," he said. "The first person I thought of was you. Not just because of your marketing skills, though those are excellent, but because of how you lead. We need someone who can build culture while driving results."

Sofia accepted the role, which came with greater responsibility, influence, and compensation. What stood out most was that she never applied for it. The opportunity found her because of her reputation as a leader who develops people and drives outcomes the right way.

"I realized that building my leadership brand was more valuable than building my technical expertise," Sofia said.

And here is the best part: the opportunities that come your way are more aligned with your values, your strengths, and your vision for your life.

You stop settling for what is available and begin pursuing what is meaningful.

You Feel the Shift Internally, Too

Leadership growth does not only show up in promotions or new roles. It shows up inside you.

You stop walking into rooms trying to prove yourself. You stop second-guessing your voice. You stop managing your image and start trusting your presence.

That is real confidence. Not the loud kind, but the grounded kind.

It is the kind that makes people lean in. The kind that frees your energy for the work that truly matters. The kind that makes you a magnet for trust and collaboration.

Priya, a senior technical leader, had struggled with imposter syndrome for years. Despite her expertise and consistent results, she constantly questioned her right to be in leadership rooms. She would over-prepare for meetings, second-guess her contributions, and often stay silent when she had valuable insights to share.

After doing her own inner work, Priya found herself in a strategic planning session where a major decision was being debated. The discussion had gone in circles for nearly an hour, with senior leaders talking past each other.

In the past, Priya would have stayed quiet, assuming others knew better. This time, she spoke up.

"I think we are missing something important here," she said. "We are debating the how without being clear on the why. What problem are we trying to solve?"

The room went silent. Then the CEO said, "That is exactly what we needed to hear. Walk us through your thinking."

Priya's question reframed the entire discussion and led to a clear, confident decision.

When asked about it later, she said, "Something was different. I was not trying to prove I belonged in that room. I just knew I had something valuable to contribute, and I trusted that it mattered."

That is the internal shift that makes external results sustainable.

Because you are no longer performing leadership. You are living it.

This Is How You Become a Leader of Choice

There are leaders people tolerate, and there are leaders people choose.

You have done the work to become the latter.

When you lead from a place of alignment, intention, and resilience, you not only expand your influence, you expand what is possible in your life and career.

Promotions, better roles, greater respect, and deeper relationships all begin to follow. You also gain the confidence to walk away from what no longer fits because you finally know your worth.

Ameena, a senior manager, learned to build her own ladder.

She had been with the same company for eight years. She was good at her job, well respected, and on track for steady promotions. But something was missing.

"I feel like I am sleepwalking through my career," she said. "I am successful by every external measure, but I do not feel fulfilled."

Over time, Ameena realized she had been climbing a ladder that did not lead where she wanted to go. She was chasing promotions and recognition in a field that did not align with her deeper values and interests.

Her company culture rewarded individual achievement over collaboration, short-term results over long-term impact, and competition over community. Ameena had succeeded in that environment, but it came at the cost of her sense of purpose.

She began to envision a different path. She wanted to lead in an environment that valued development, sustainable growth, and positive impact.

Instead of continuing to climb the existing ladder, Ameena started building her own.

She began networking with purpose-driven organizations. She volunteered for leadership roles that reflected her values. She built new expertise in areas that energized her rather than those that only advanced her title.

Two years later, she was recruited for a leadership role at a company that matched her vision. The work was more meaningful, the culture was healthier, and the compensation was stronger.

"I stopped asking, 'How do I get promoted?' and started asking, 'How do I create the kind of career I actually want?'" Ameena said. "That question changed everything."

This is how you become a leader of choice. You do not wait to be chosen. You choose yourself first.

Your Turn: Tools to Amplify Your Impact

These tools help you strategically leverage the leadership foundation you've built to create expanded opportunities and influence.

Tool 23: Your Opportunity Filter

Purpose: To help you evaluate opportunities through a lens of clarity and alignment so you can say yes with intention and no without guilt.

Instructions:

Step 1: Define your criteria. Choose three to five that matter most when considering a new opportunity.

Examples include:

- Aligns with my core values
- Develops my leadership in a meaningful way
- Expands my visibility or strategic impact
- Protects time for my priorities
- Energizes me rather than drains me

Step 2: Score each opportunity. When a project, role, or partnership arises, rate it on a scale of one to five against each criterion.

Step 3: Decide with intention. If it does not score high on the things that matter most, it is probably not your next best move.

Mirror Move: Use your filter transparently and model it for others. The next time you receive an opportunity, talk through our reasoning. You might say:

"I have developed a set of criteria for evaluating new opportunities. Here is how this one aligns."

If you decline, explain with clarity: "This does not align with my current focus on [criterion], but here is another way I can support you."

Share your process with your team: "Here is how I think about opportunities. What criteria matter most to you?"

This shows others how to make thoughtful choices and encourages them to define what alignment means for themselves.

Tool 24: Future You Mapping

Purpose: To visualize your next level of leadership and identify the actions that will move you toward it.

Instructions: Imagine it is two years from now and you are thriving in a role that feels like a natural next step. You are respected, energized, and making an impact.

Reflect or journal on the following questions:

- What do you do every day that feels meaningful?

- Who are you working with, and how are they growing because of your leadership?

- What problems are you trusted to solve?

- What kinds of decisions do you have a seat at the table for?

- What feedback do you hear from others?

Now ask yourself: What would future me thank present me for doing right now?

Use the answer to identify one bold next step.

Mirror Move: Share your vision and ask for guidance. Choose one person who could help you move toward your vision. This might be a mentor, senior leader, or trusted peer.

Share your reflection with them:

- "Here is what I am envisioning for my next chapter."

- "What opportunities or experiences do you think would help me get there?"

- "How can I better position myself for this kind of impact?"

- "Will you help me stay accountable to this goal?"

Then take one concrete action based on their advice within two weeks.

Tool 25: The Leadership Brand Statement

Purpose: To clearly articulate the unique value you bring as a leader.

Instructions: Complete this statement:

"I am a leader who [unique approach] to help [target audience] achieve [outcomes] by [specific methods or values]."

Examples:

- "I am a leader who combines strategic thinking with genuine care to help emerging leaders achieve breakthrough performance by creating environments where people can take risks and learn from failure."

- "I am a leader who uses data-driven insight and collaborative decision-making to help teams achieve complex goals by building trust and alignment across diverse perspectives."

Refine your statement until it feels authentic, specific, and powerful.

Mirror Move: Test and refine your brand through feedback. Share your statement with five people who know your leadership well: a boss, a peer, a direct report, someone from another department, and a mentor.

Ask:

- "Does this sound true to how you experience my leadership?"

- "What would you add or adjust?"

- "Where have you seen this brand in action?"

Refine your statement based on what you learn, then use it to guide how you evaluate opportunities, communicate your value, and show up every day.

Final Thoughts: Unlock Your Future

Leadership growth is not only about being better. It is about unlocking the next level of your confidence, your career, and your choices.

You have done the internal work.
Now the external results begin to align.

This is the moment when your impact grows and your options multiply.
The foundation you have built through self-awareness, reclaimed energy, intentional culture, and authentic influence has become your platform for expanded impact.

You are not the same leader who began this journey.
You are more grounded.
More intentional.
More resilient.
More influential.

The world needs leaders who have done the work to lead with purpose.
Leaders who understand that real influence comes from character, not charisma.
Leaders who know that sustainable success is built on lifting others up, not climbing over them.

You are that kind of leader now.
Your growth is not only good for you.
It is good for everyone whose life you will touch through your leadership.

So, step into that bigger version of yourself.
Take the stretch opportunities.
Build the career that reflects your values and vision.
Lead like it matters.

Because it does.

CHAPTER NINE

The Mirror Never Leaves You

You have done the work. You have looked inward. You have led outward.

But before we close this book, there is something important to remember: the journey does not end here. This kind of work is not something you finish. It is something you return to, again and again.

Leadership is not a finish line. It is a practice, a rhythm, and a recalibration. It is the act of looking back into the mirror when things feel off, because now you know better than to power through blindly.

The mirror you have been using is not an object that sits on your desk or hangs on a wall. It lives in how you show up, in how you catch yourself mid-reaction, and in how you make the next best decision. Not always the perfect one, but the one that aligns with who you want to be.

You Are the Leadership Mirror Now

You have learned that leadership is not a title, a set of tools, or a persona you put on for meetings. It is not an act. It is not performance. It is not the loudest voice or the best presentation deck.

Leadership is who you are. It is what people feel in your presence. It is the ripple you create in a room. It is how your team grows or shrinks under your care. It is what you model when things go sideways. It is how you own the mess and still choose to lead.

You have examined your patterns, not just the easy ones. You have reclaimed your time and your energy and stopped treating burnout like a badge of honor. You have faced hard truths about the culture you create and taken ownership of your impact. You have built influence through trust, not force, and it shows. You have chosen growth over guilt, clarity over chaos, and people are watching. They are learning.

In doing that, you have walked the full arc of The Leadership Mirror Framework. You have looked inward with honesty, reset how you manage your time and energy, shaped the culture within your span of control, expanded your influence, led through the cracks, and begun to live your legacy in real time. That is not theory. That is practiced, embodied leadership.

You have done what many leaders have never done. You have paused, reflected, and shifted. You have built a foundation no one can take from you. That changes everything.

This journey gives you more than tools. It gives you awareness, courage, and the ability to course-correct quickly when you drift. And you will drift. We all do. That is not failure. That is being human.

The mirror is not there to judge you. It is there to guide you back to who you want to be.

The Impact That Outlasts the Moment

You do not need to be perfect to make an impact. You just need to be real.

People do not follow perfection. They follow presence. They follow humility. They follow courage and care.

They follow leaders who can say, "I got that wrong," or "I am still learning," or "Let us figure this out together." They follow the ones who stay when things are hard, who choose integrity over image, who do not hide behind authority but lead as human beings.

That is the kind of leader the world needs. That is the kind of leader you are becoming. That is the legacy you are already living.

I think about Linda from Chapter Five, the receiving clerk with no formal authority but tremendous influence. Linda understood something many titled leaders miss: legacy is not about position. It is about impact.

Every day, she chose to see people, to care about their experience, to make their work life a little better. She did not wait until retirement to start building her legacy. She lived it in every interaction.

You do not wait until your last day on the job to have a legacy. You live it every day in your choices, your presence, and your impact.

Now It Is Your Turn to Multiply

As we move forward, the work becomes even more meaningful.

You aren't just becoming a better leader yourself but becoming the kind of leader who builds other leaders.

It starts with a question: who around you needs a mirror?

Who is doubting themselves and just needs one person to believe in them? Who is hungry for feedback they have never received? Who is longing for a different kind of leadership than what they have experienced?

Be that person. Be the one who sees the gap and steps into it with grace. Be the one who calls people forward, not out. Be the one who says, "I have been there too, and here is what helped me."

Hold the mirror up, not to criticize, but to challenge, inspire, and guide. That is how you expand your impact. That is how you multiply. That is how you create a ripple that outlasts your presence.

Hector, a manufacturing supervisor, learned how to build a multiplier mindset. He had transformed his own leadership using the principles in this book, moving from reactive and controlling to respected and trusted. But Hector did not stop there.

He saw his peers struggling with the same things he once faced, and he started sharing what had helped him. He had coffee conversations. He passed on tools and stories. He offered to listen when others faced tough moments.

Within a year, the entire supervisory team had grown stronger. Turnover dropped. Quality improved. Engagement rose. Hector had multiplied his impact by developing other leaders.

"I realized that keeping what I learned did not serve anyone," he said. "When I started helping others grow, my own leadership got stronger."

That is the multiplier effect. When you develop others, you reinforce your own growth and expand your influence exponentially.

The Work Never Ends. That Is the Gift.

There will be days when you forget. Moments when the old patterns return like a familiar song. Seasons when progress feels slow and clarity feels far away.

Do not let that discourage you. That is not failure. That is the path.

Real growth is not linear. It is layered. It loops until the learning sticks.

A leader I once worked with thought they had arrived at consistent effectiveness. Then came a new role, a difficult team, and unrealistic expectations. Under pressure, the old habits returned. Control. Defensiveness. Overdrive.

Their first reaction was frustration. *I should know better by now.*

But instead of judgment, they chose reflection. They asked, *What is triggering these old patterns? What do I need to recalibrate? How can I return to my best self?*

That reflection became the breakthrough. They discovered that growth is not about never slipping back. It is about noticing faster, recovering sooner, and learning more deeply each time.

Even now, I find myself pausing before a tough conversation, taking a breath, and asking, *What kind of leader do I want to be in this moment?* That is what the mirror gives you: choice.

So when you find yourself in one of those moments, do not reach for perfection. Reach for honesty. Reach for presence. Reach for the mirror.

Your Turn: Tools for Lifelong Leadership Growth

These final tools help you maintain and continue your leadership development journey beyond this book.

Tool 26: The Mirror Check-In Map

Purpose: Turn reflection into a recurring habit that keeps you aligned with the leader you want to be.

Instructions: Pick one consistent time each week. Use this 5-minute check-in to stay on track.

Ask yourself:

- Where did I lead from my best self this week? (When did I pause, choose clarity over reaction, show up as the best leader I want to be?)

- Where did I drift off track? (When did I react, avoid, or compromise my values?)

- What impact did I create? (Think about the ripple effect, the tone you set, what people felt after being around you.)

- Does this align with who I want to be known as? (Are my actions matching the legacy I want to live?)

- What one thing will I adjust next week? (Keep it simple. One shift, one focus.)

- Write it down or record a voice memo. Don't overthink it. Just notice.

Why it matters: This isn't about perfection. It's about staying awake to your impact and course-correcting quickly when you drift.

Mirror Move: Share your weekly check-in with someone you trust. Pick a colleague, mentor, or friend and say, "I'm doing a weekly leadership reflection. Can I share what I'm noticing with you once a month?" Having someone else hear your insights makes you more honest with yourself and creates accountability for the changes you want to make.

Tool 27: The Learning Sprint

Purpose: Tackle one specific leadership challenge with focused intensity over 30 days.

Instructions: Pick Your Challenge: What one leadership issue is costing you right now? Where are you stuck, reactive, or avoiding something important?

30-Day Sprint Process:

- Days 1-7: Research and gather input.

- Days 8-21: Practice and test new approaches.

- Days 22-30: Refine, embed, and make it a habit.

End of Sprint: Write down what you learned, what you'll keep doing, and what your next sprint will focus on.

Why it matters: Most leadership development happens in slow motion. This gives you focused progress on the stuff that's holding you back.

Mirror Move: Tell your team what you are working on. Say, "I am focusing on getting better at [specific skill]. You may see me trying new things. I welcome your feedback." Transparency builds trust and models continuous learning. This transparency shows your team that leaders never stop learning and gives you real-time feedback on your progress.

Tool 28: The 360 Reality Check

Purpose: Get honest feedback about your leadership impact from multiple perspectives every quarter.

Instructions: Pick four or five people who see your leadership from different angles and ask them three questions:

- What am I doing well that works?

- What could I change to be more effective?
- What blind spot might I have that would help me to see?

Look for patterns. Pick one strength to amplify and one area to improve. Then thank everyone and tell them what you plan to do next.

Why it matters: You cannot see yourself the way others see you. This helps you understand your real impact.

Mirror Move: Close the loop publicly. Tell your team what you heard and how you plan to grow. Say, "I asked for feedback. Here is what I learned and how I am adjusting." That kind of openness builds trust and shows your commitment to learning.

One Last Look

Before you put this book down, take one more look in the mirror. Not to judge. Not to critique. But to acknowledge.

You have come a long way. You have done real work. You have told yourself the truth. You have started leading in a way that feels aligned with who you really are.

You are not the same leader who started this book. You are clearer, more grounded, more intentional, and more capable than ever before.

And when you drift, you now know how to return. You know how to look in the mirror without flinching. You know how to course-correct when you lose your footing. You know how to lead from the inside out.

Keep leading. Keep growing. Keep showing others what is possible when you lead this way.

Because the mirror is not something you look into. It is something you carry with you. It lives in how you show up, how you decide, and how you lead today, tomorrow, and every day after.

The mirror never leaves you. And that is exactly the point.

The Journey: Where You've Been and Where You're Going

As we close, take a moment to see the whole path you have traveled.

You began by looking inward, discovering who you are as a leader and what truly drives you. You learned to manage your inner world, reclaim your time and energy, design culture with intention, grow your influence, lead through the cracks, and live your legacy in real time.

Each chapter added another layer to The Leadership Mirror Framework and to you: more clarity, more courage, more confidence. Each tool strengthened your ability to lead with integrity and awareness, not performance and pretense.

Now you are equipped to continue without this book in your hands. The real work happens in your next conversation, your next decision, your next ripple.

Final Thoughts: Your Leadership Ripple Effect

Your impact reaches further than you can see. Every person you lead carries forward what they learn from you. Every culture you shape influences how others show up long after you are gone. Every decision made from integrity creates ripples that change lives.

The world needs leaders who do this kind of work. Leaders who have the courage to look inward before leading outward.

Leaders who understand that power grows through service. Leaders who choose alignment over ambition and legacy over ego.

You are that leader now.

The mirror will always be there, showing you what you need to see when you need to see it. Sometimes it will reflect your growth. Sometimes it will reveal what still needs attention. Always, it will remind you that leadership begins within.

You have learned to look. You have learned to lead. Now it is time to live what you have learned.

You started this book tired of performing leadership. You arrive here ready to live it, in a way that is sustainable for you and transformational for the people you lead.

The mirror never leaves you. And neither does your potential to create change that matters.

Your journey continues. Your impact multiplies. Your legacy lives.

Lead on.

The Leadership Mirror Companion Workbook

The complete worksheet companion for all 28 tools is available as a free download at:

www.theleadershipmirror.com

Each worksheet corresponds to one of the 28 tools in the book. Print what you need, share with your team, and return to them as your leadership grows.

Acknowledgments

This book may have my name on the cover, but it was shaped by countless moments, conversations, and people who challenged me to look inward long before I ever asked others to do the same.

To the leaders I have worked with over the years, thank you. You trusted me with your reality, not just your results. You let me see the pressure, the uncertainty, and the decisions that do not show up on org charts or dashboards. This work exists because of you. In many ways, you have been the mirror as much as I have.

To the mentors, peers, and collaborators who pushed my thinking, challenged my assumptions, and refused to let me stay at the surface, thank you for making this work stronger. You know who you are. The conversations we have had, and continue to have, are woven throughout these pages.

To those who helped bring this book to life behind the scenes, including editors, reviewers, and early readers, thank you for your honesty and your patience. You did not just help refine the words; you helped sharpen the message.

To my friends and family, thank you for the support you give in ways that often go unseen. Writing a book does not just take time; it takes presence, energy, and space. You gave me all three.

And finally, to anyone willing to look in the mirror, even when it would be easier not to, this work is for you.

References

Brown, B. (2018). Dare to lead: Brave work. Tough conversations. Whole hearts. Random House.

Clear, J. (2018). Atomic habits: An easy & proven way to build good habits & break bad ones. Avery.

David, S. (2016). Emotional agility: Get unstuck, embrace change, and thrive in work and life. Avery.

Dweck, C. S. (2006). Mindset: The new psychology of success. Random House.

Edmondson, A. (2019). The fearless organization: Creating psychological safety in the workplace for learning, innovation, and growth. Wiley.

Goleman, D. (1995). Emotional intelligence: Why it can matter more than IQ. Bantam Books.

Hanson, R. (2013). Hardwiring happiness: The new brain science of contentment, calm, and confidence. Harmony Books.

Kouzes, J. M., & Posner, B. Z. (2017). The leadership challenge (6th ed.). Wiley.

Kross, E. (2021). Chatter: The voice in our head, why it matters, and how to harness it. Crown.

152

About the Author

Julie McManus is a leadership strategist, executive coach, and creator of *The Leadership Mirror*—a practical framework that helps leaders move from daily chaos to calm, focused leadership that drives sustainable results.

With more than four decades of experience leading operational, cultural, and change initiatives across five continents, Julie has partnered with Fortune 500 organizations and executive teams to strengthen engagement, streamline operations, and execute complex, multi-million-dollar transformations. Her background spans executive leadership, global consulting, supply chain strategy, and organizational development—giving her both operational credibility and deep human insight.

But Julie's work goes deeper than strategy. She believes leadership is an inside job. Through executive coaching, facilitation, and enterprise transformation, she helps leaders confront blind spots, manage their energy, and intentionally shape the cultures around them. Her approach turns clarity into a daily discipline, trust into a measurable asset, and accountability into a system—not a slogan.

Known for her grounded presence and practical tools, Julie equips leaders to build capacity, protect culture, and multiply healthy leadership. She lives in Ohio and partners with leaders ready to look inward—so they can lead outward with integrity and impact.

www.ingramcontent.com/pod-product-compliance
Lightning Source LLC
Chambersburg PA
CBHW022051050726
47591CB00002B/497